OCCULT CHEMISTRY

OCCULT CHEMISTRY

BY
ANNIE BESANT
CURUPPUMULLAGE JINARAJADASA

GYAN

ISBN: 978-81-212-1876-4 (HB)
First Published, 1908
Published, 2018
Published by

Gyan Publishing House
5, Ansari Road
Daryaganj, New Delhi-110002
Phone: 011-47034999, 9811692060
www.gyanbooks.com
E-mail: books@gyanbooks.com

Printed at: G. Print Process, Delhi.

FOREWORD.

This is an excursion into a hitherto unoccupied field, and is offered merely as a series of careful observations, subject to correction by fuller and repeated investigations.

The articles are reprinted from the *Theosophist*, and in a few cases on the early pages, as on page 15, the reference to the pages of the magazine was unfortunately not corrected. We should be much obliged, if any errors are noted in the text or diagrams, that they should be forwarded to Adyar, in order that they may be corrected, should a new edition of the book be required. On page 28, line 8, for *helium* read *occultum*.

Adyar,
December 7th, 1908.

CONTENTS.

		PAGE.
ARTICLE	I—Introductory	1
ARTICLE	II—Groupings	11
ARTICLE	III—The Dumb-bell Group	15
ARTICLE	IV—Dissociations	25
ARTICLE	V—The Tetrahedral Groups	33
ARTICLE	VI—Dissociations	43
ARTICLE	VII—The Cube Groups	50
ARTICLE	VIII—Dissociations	59
ARTICLE	IX—The Octohedral Bars and Spike Groups ...	64
ARTICLE	X—Dissociations	77
ARTICLE	XI—The Star Group	83
ARTICLE	XII—Radium	89
APPENDIX	—The Æther of Space	i
	—*Lucifer* article of November 1895	xi
	—The Platonic Solids	xx
	—Notes	xxi

OCCULT CHEMISTRY.

IT may be remembered that an article, bearing the above title, appeared in *Lucifer*, November 1895, and was reprinted as a separate pamphlet in 1905. In that article three chemical elements —hydrogen, oxygen and nitrogen—were clairvoyantly examined, and their analyses were presented tentatively to the public. The work was done by Mr. Leadbeater and myself. The pressing nature of our other labors prevented further investigation at the time, but we have, however, lately had the opportunity of pursuing these researches further, and as a considerable amount of work has been done, it seems worth while, still tentatively, to report the observations made. Certain principles seem to emerge from the mass of details, and it is possible that readers, who are better versed in chemistry than ourselves, may see suggestions to which we are blind. An observer's duty is to state clearly his observations ; it is for others to judge of their value, and to decide whether they indicate lines of research that may be profitably followed up by scientists.

The drawings of the elements were done by two Theosophical artists, Herr Hecker and Mrs. Kirby, whom we sincerely thank ; the diagrams, showing the details of the construction of each " element," we owe to the most painstaking labor of Mr. Jinarâjaḍâsa, without whose aid it would have been impossible for us to have presented clearly and definitely the complicated arrangements by which the chemical elements are built up. We have also to thank him for a number of most useful notes, implying much careful research, which are incorporated in the present series, and without which I could not have written these papers. Lastly, we have to thank Sir William Crookes for kindly lending his diagram of the grouping of the elements, showing them as arranged on successive "figures of eight," a grouping which, as will be seen, receives much support from clairvoyant observations.

As we study these complex arrangements, we realise the truth of the old Platonic idea that the LOGOS geometrises: and we recall H. P. Blavatsky's statement that nature ever builds by form and number.

The method of examination employed was that of clairvoyance; there were only two observers—Mr. Leadbeater and myself—and it is very desirable that our results should be tested by others who can use the same extension of physical sight. The researches being carried on upon the physical plane—the forms examined being gaseous and etheric only—a very slight intensification of ordinary vision is all that is necessary, and many should, therefore, be able to test our observations. They cannot be regarded as established, by the outside world, until others have corroborated them; and we put them forward in the hope of stimulating work along this line, and of thus bringing to science, when its instruments fail it, the old, old instrument of enlarged human vision.

The first difficulty that faced us was the identification of the forms seen on focussing the sight on gases. We could only proceed tentatively. Thus, a very common form in the air had a sort of dumb-bell shape (see Plate I); we examined this, comparing our rough sketches, and counted its atoms; these, divided by 18—the number of ultimate atoms in hydrogen—gave us 23·22 as atomic weight, and this offered the presumption that it was sodium. We then took various substances—common salt, etc.—in which we knew sodium was present, and found the dumb-bell form in all. In other cases, we took small fragments of metals, as iron, tin, zinc, silver, gold; in others, again, pieces of ore, mineral waters, etc., etc., and, for the rarest substances, Mr. Leadbeater visited a mineralogical museum, a few miles off. In all, 57 chemical elements were examined, out of the 78 recognised by modern chemistry.

In addition to these, we found 3 chemical waifs: an unrecognised stranger between hydrogen and helium which we named occultum, for purposes of reference, and 2 varieties of one element, which we named kalon and meta-kalon, between xenon and osmium; we also found 4 varieties of 4 recognised elements and prefixed meta to the name of each, and a second form of platinum, that we named

PLATE I.

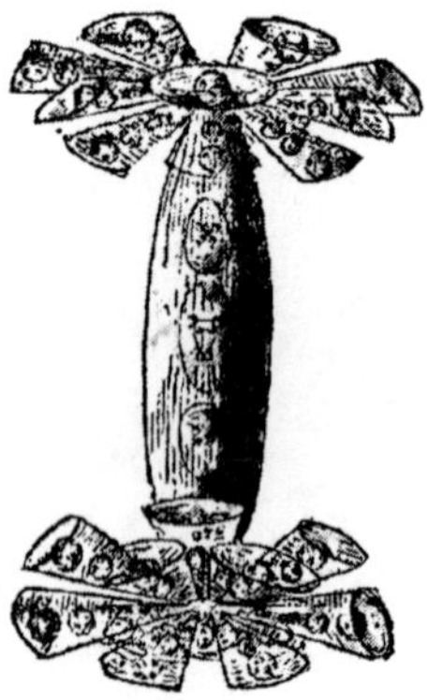

SODIUM.

Pt. B. Thus, we have tabulated in all 65 chemical elements, or chemical atoms, completing three of Sir William Crookes' lemniscates, sufficient for some amount of generalisation.

In counting the number of ultimate atoms in a chemical elemental atom, we did not count them throughout, one by one; when, for instance, we counted up the ultimate atoms in sodium, we dictated the number in each convenient group to Mr. Jinarâjadâsa, and he multiplied out the total, divided by 18, and announced the result. Thus: sodium (see Plate I.) is composed of an upper part, divisible into a globe and 12 funnels, a lower part, similarly divided; and a connecting rod. We counted the number in the upper part: globe—10; the number in two or three of the funnels—each 16; the number of funnels—12; the same for the lower part; in the connecting rod—14. Mr. Jinarâjadâsa reckoned: $10 + (16 \times 12) = 202$; hence: $202 + 202 + 14 = 418$: divided by $18 = 23{\cdot}22$ recurring. By this method we guarded our counting from any pre-possession, as it was impossible for us to know how the various numbers would result on addition, multiplication and division, and the exciting moment came when we waited to see if our results endorsed or approached any accepted weight. In the heavier elements, such as gold, with 3546 atoms, it would have been impossible to count each atom without quite unnecessary waste of time, when making a preliminary investigation. Later, it may be worth while to count each division separately, as in some we noticed that two groups, at first sight alike, differed by 1 or 2 atoms, and some very slight errors may, in this way, have crept into our calculations.

In the following table is a list of the chemical elements examined; the first column gives the names, the asterisk affixed to some indicating that they have not yet been discovered by orthodox chemistry. The second column gives the number of ultimate physical atoms contained in one chemical atom of the element concerned. The third column gives the weight as compared with hydrogen, taken as 18, and this is obtained by dividing the calculated number of ultimate atoms by 18. The fourth column gives the recognised weight-number, mostly according to the latest list of atomic weights, the "International List" of 1905, given in Erdmann's *Lehrbuch der Anorganischen Chemie.* These weights differ from those hitherto accepted, and are generally lighter than those given in earlier textbooks. It is interesting to note that our counting endorses the earlier numbers, for the most part, and we must wait to see if later observations will endorse the last results of orthodox chemistry, or confirm ours.

Hydrogen	18	1	1
* Occultum	54	3	....
Helium	72	4	3·94
Lithium	127	7·06	6·98
Baryllium	164	9·11	9·01
Boron	200	11·11	10·86
Carbon	216	12	11·91
Nitrogen	261	14·50	14·01
Oxygen	290	16·11	15·879
Fluorine	340	18·88	18·90
Neon	360	20	19·9
* Meta-Neon	402	22·33	..
Sodium	418	23·22	22·88
Magnesium	432	24	24 18
Aluminium	486	27	26·91
Silicon	520	28 88	28 18
Phosphorus	558	31	30·77
Sulphur	576	32	31 82
Chlorine	639	35·50	35·473
Potassium	701	38·944	38·85
Argon	714	39·66	39·60
Calcium	720	40	39·74
* Metargon	756	42	..
Scandium	792	44	43 78
Titanium	864	48	47·74
Vanadium	918	51	50·84
Chromium	936	52	51 74
Manganese	992	55·11	54·57
Iron	1008	56	55·47
Cobalt	1036	57·55	57·7
Nickel	1064	59·11	58·30
Copper	1139	63·277	63.12
Zinc	1170	65	64·91
Gallium	1260	70	69·50
Germanium	1300	72·22	71·93
Arsenic	1350	75	74·45
Selenium	1422	79	78·58
Bromine	1439	79·944	79·953
Krypton	1464	81·33	81·20
* Meta-Krypton	1506	83·66	...
Rubidium	1530	85	84·85
Strontium	1568	87·11	86 95
Yttrium	1606	89·22	88·34
Zirconium	1624	90·22	89·85
Niobium	1719	95·50	93 25
Molybdenum...	1746	97	95 26
Ruthenium	1848	102·66	100·91
Rhodium	1876	104·22	102·23
Palladium	1904	105·77	105·74
Silver	1945	108·055	107·93
Cadmium	2016	112	111·60
Indium	2052	114	114·05
Tin	2024	118	118·10
Antimony	2169	120·50	119·34

PLATE II.

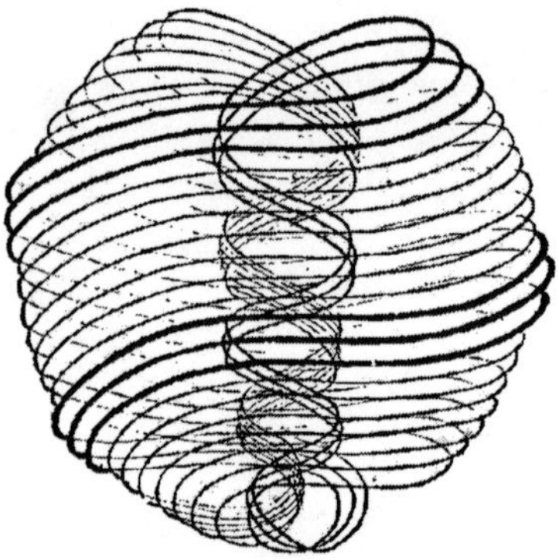

MALE.

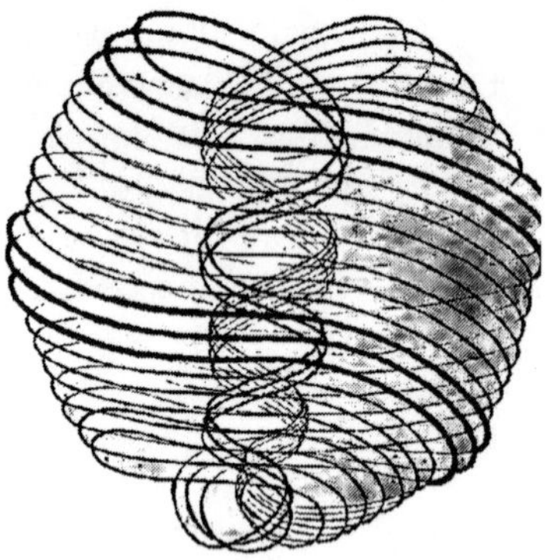

FEMALE.

Tellurium ...	2223	123·50	126·64
Iodine ...	2287	127·055	126·01
Xenon ...	2298	127·66	127·10
* Meta-Xenon ...	2340	130	...
* Kalon ...	3054	169·66	...
* Meta-Kalon ...	3096	172	...
Osmium ...	3430	190·55	189·55
Iridium ...	3458	192·11	191·56
Platinum A ...	3486	193·66	193·34
* Platinum B ...	3514	195·22	...
Gold ...	3546	197	195·74

As the words "ultimate physical atom" must frequently occur, it is necessary to state what we mean by the phrase. Any gaseous chemical atom may be dissociated into less complicated bodies; these, again, into still less complicated; these, again, into yet still less complicated. These will be dealt with presently. After the third dissociation but one more is possible; the fourth dissociation gives the ultimate physical atom.* This may vanish from the physical plane, but it can undergo no further dissociation on it. In this ultimate state of physical matter two types of atoms have been observed; they are alike in everything save the direction of their whorls and of the force which pours through them. In the one case force pours in from the 'outside,' from fourth-dimensional space,† and passing through the atom, pours into the physical world. In the second, it pours in from the physical world, and out through the atom into the 'outside' again,† *i.e.*, vanishes from the physical world. The one is like a spring, from which water bubbles out; the other is like a hole, into which water disappears. We call the atoms from which force comes out *positive*, or *male*; those through which it disappears, *negative* or *female*. All atoms, so far as observed, are of one or other of these two forms. (Plate II.)

It will be seen that the atom is a sphere, slightly flattened, and there is a depression at the point where the force flows in, causing a heart-like form. Each atom is surrounded by a field, formed of the atoms of the four higher planes, which surround and interpenetrate it.

The atom can scarcely be said to be a 'thing,' though it is the material out of which all things physical are composed. It is

* The atomic sub-plane.

† The astral plane.

formed by the flow of the life-force * and vanishes with its ebb. When this force arises in 'space' †—the apparent void which must be filled with subtance of some kind, of inconceivable tenuity—atoms appear; if this be artificially stopped for a single atom, the atom disappears; there is nothing left. Presumably were that flow checked but for an instant, the whole physical world would vanish, as a cloud melts away in the empyrean. It is only the persistence of that flow ‡ which maintains the physical basis of the universe. §

In order to examine the construction of the atom, a space is artificially made ‖; then, if an opening be made in the wall thus constructed, the surrounding force flows in, and three whorls immediately appear, surrounding the 'hole' with their triple spiral of two and a half coils, and returning to their origin by a spiral within the atom; these are at once followed by seven finer whorls, which following the spiral of the first three on the outer surface, and returning to their origin by a spiral within that, flowing in the opposite direction—form a caduceus with the first three. Each of the three coarser whorls, flattened out, makes a closed circle; each of the seven finer ones, similarly flattened out, makes a closed circle. The forces which flow in them, again, come from 'outside,' from a fourth-dimensional space. ¶ Each of the finer whorls is formed of seven yet finer ones, set successively at right angles to each other, each finer than its predecessor; these we call spirillæ.¶¶

It will be understood from the foregoing, that the atom cannot be said to have a wall of its own, unless these whorls of force can be so designated; its 'wall' is the pressed back 'space.' As said in 1895, of the chemical atom, the force " clears itself a space,

---

* Known to Theosophists as Fohat, the force of which all the physical plane forces—electricities—are differentiations.

† When Fohat " digs holes in space."

‡ The first life-wave, the work of the third Logos.

§ A māyā, truly.

‖ By a certain action of the will, known to students, it is possible to make such a space, by pressing back and walling off the matter of space.

¶ Again the astral world.

¶¶ Each spirilla is animated by the life-force of a plane, and four are at present normally active, one for each round. Their activity in an individual may be prematurely forced by yoga practice.

pressing back the undifferentiated matter of the plane, and making to itself a whirling wall of this matter." The wall belongs to space, not to the atom.

In the three whorls flow currents of different electricities ; the seven vibrate in response to etheric waves of all kinds—to sound, light, heat, etc. ; they show the seven colors of the spectrum ; give out the seven sounds of the natural scale ; respond in a variety of ways to physical vibration—flashing, singing, pulsing bodies, they move incessantly, inconceivably beautiful and brilliant.*

The atom has—as observed so far—three proper motions, *i.e.*, motions of its own, independent of any imposed upon it from outside. It turns incessantly upon its own axis, spinning like a top; it describes a small circle with its axis, as though the axis of the spinning top moved in a small circle ; it has a regular pulsation, a contraction and expansion, like the pulsation of the heart. When a force is brought to bear upon it, it dances up and down, flings itself wildly from side to side, performs the most astonishing and rapid gyrations, but the three fundamental motions incessantly persist. If it be made to vibrate, as a whole, at the rate which gives any one of the seven colors, the whorl belonging to that color glows out brilliantly.

An electric current brought to bear upon the atoms checks their proper motions, *i.e.*, renders them slower ; the atoms exposed to it arrange themselves in parallel lines, and in each line the heart-shaped depression receives the flow, which passes out through the apex into the depression of the next, and so on. The atoms always set themselves to the current. The well-known division of diamagnetic and paramagnetic depends generally on this fact, or on an analogous action on molecules, as may be seen in the accompanying diagrams.†

---

* "The ten numbers of the sun. These are called Dis—in reality space—the forces spread in space, three of which are contained in the Sun's Atman, or seventh principle, and seven are the rays shot out by the Sun." The atom is a sun in miniature in its own universe of the inconceivably minute. Each of the seven whorls is connected with one of the Planetary Logoi, so that each Planetary Logos has a direct influence playing on the very matter of which all things are constructed. It may be supposed that the three, conveying electricity, a differentiation of Fohat, are related to the Solar Logoi.

† The action of electricity opens up ground of large extent, and cannot be dealt with here. Does it act on the atoms themselves, or on molecules, or sometimes on

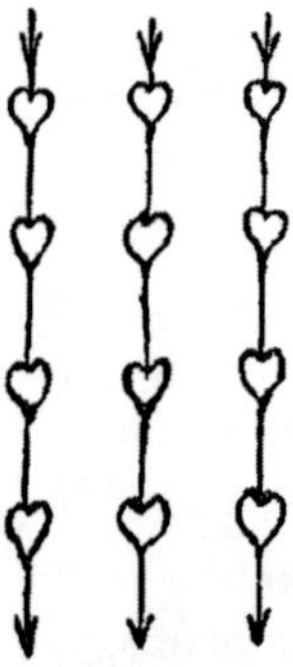

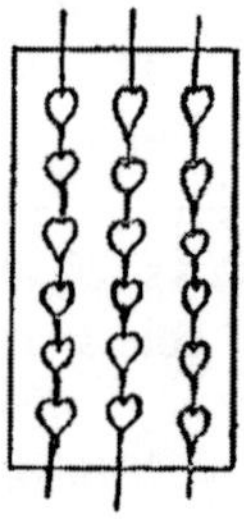

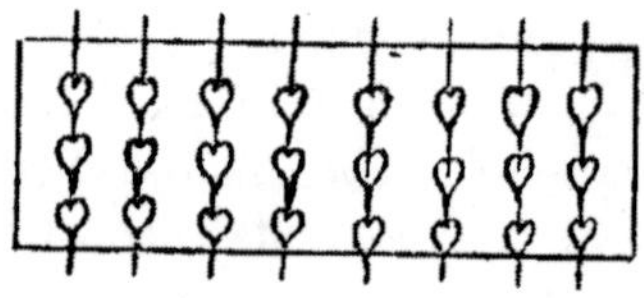

Two atoms, positive and negative, brought near to each other, attract each other, and then commence to revolve round each other, forming a relatively stable duality ; such a molecule is neutral. Combinations of three or more atoms are positive, negative or neutral, according to the internal molecular arrangement ; the neutral are relatively stable, the positive and negative are continually in search of their respective opposites, with a view to establishing a relatively permanent union.

Three states of matter exist between the atomic state and the gaseous—the state in which the chemical atoms are found, the recognised chemical elements ; for our purposes we may ignore the liquid and solid states. For the sake of clearness and brevity in description, we have been obliged to name these states ; we call the atomic state of the chemist *elemental ;* the state which results from breaking up chemical elements, *proto-elemental ;* the next higher, *meta-proto-elemental ;* the next higher, *hyper-meta-proto-elemental ;* then comes the atomic state. These are briefly marked as El., Proto., Meta., and Hyper.*

The simplest unions of atoms, never, apparently consisting of more than seven, form the first molecular state of physical matter.

Here are some characteristic combinations of the Hyper state ;

---

one and sometimes on the other ? In soft iron, for instance, are the internal arrangements of the chemical atom forcibly distorted, and do they elastically return to their original relations when released ? and in steel is the distortion permanent ? In all the diagrams the heart shaped body, exaggerated to show the depression caused by the inflow and the point caused by the outflow, is a single atom.

* These sub-planes are familiar to the Theosophist as gaseous, etheric, super-etheric, sub-atomic, atomic ; or as Gas, Ether 4, Ether 3, Ether 2, Ether 1.

the atom is conventional, with the depression emphasised; the lines, always entering at the depression and coming out at the apex, show the resultants of lines of force; where no line appears entering the depression, the force wells up from fourth-dimensional space; where no line appears leaving the apex, the force disappears into fourth-dimensional space; where the point of entry and departure is outside the atoms, it is indicated by a dot.*

TYPES OF HYPER-META-PROTO-ELEMENTAL MATTER.

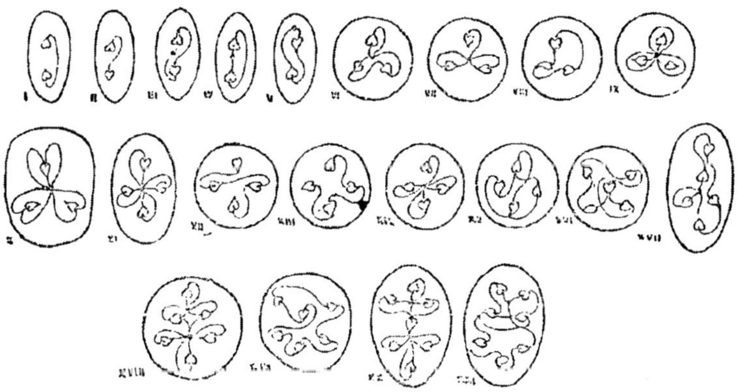

The molecules show all kinds of possible combinations; the combinations spin, turn head over heels, and gyrate in endless ways. Each aggregation is surrounded with an apparent cell-wall, the circle or oval, due to the pressure on the surrounding matter caused by its whirling motion; they strike on each other † and rebound, dart hither and thither, for reasons we have not distinguished.

The Meta state, in some of its combinations, appears at first sight to repeat those of the Hyper state; the only obvious way of distinguishing to which some of the molecules of less complexity belong is to pull them out of the "cell-wall;" if they are Hyper molecules they at once fly off as separate atoms; if they are Hyper-Meta molecules they break up into two or more molecules containing a smaller number of atoms. Thus one of the Meta molecules of iron, containing seven atoms, is identical in appearance with a Hyper heptad, but the latter dissociates into

* It must be remembered that the diagrams represent three-dimensional objects, and the atoms are not all on a plane, necessarily.

† That is, the surrounding magnetic fields strike on each other.

seven atoms, the former into two triads and a single atom. Long-continued research into the detailed play of forces and their results is necessary; we are here only able to give preliminary facts and details—are opening up the way. The following may serve as characteristic Meta types:

TYPES OF META-PROTO-ELEMENTAL MATTER.

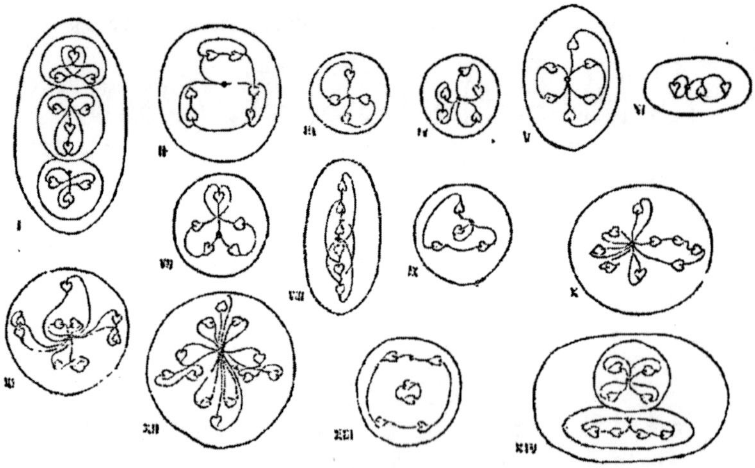

These are taken from constituents of the various elements; 1 from Gl; 2 and 3 from Fe; 4 from Bo; 5, 6 and 7 from C; 8 from He; 9 from Fl; 10, 11, 12 from Li; 13 and 14 from Na. Others will be seen in the course of breaking up the elements.

The Proto state preserves many of the forms in the elements, modified by release from the pressure to which they are subjected in the chemical atom. In this state various groups are thus recognisable which are characteristic of allied metals.

TYPES ON PROTO-ELEMENTAL MATTER.

These are taken from the products of the first disintegration of the chemical atom, by forcibly removing it from its hole. The groups fly apart, assuming a great variety of forms often more or less geometrical; the lines between the constituents of the groups, where indicated, no longer represent lines of force, but are intended to represent the impression of form, *i.e.*, of the relative position and motion of the constituents, made on the mind of the observer. They

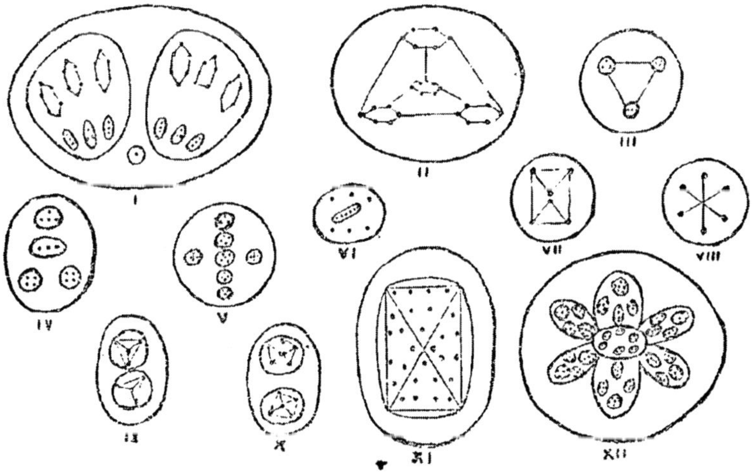

are illusive, for there are no lines, but the appearance of lines is caused by the rapid motion of the constituents up and down, or along them backwards and forwards. The dots represent atoms, or groups of atoms, within the proto elements. 1 is found in C ; 2 and 3 in He ; 4 in Fl ; 5 in Li ; 6 in N ; 7 in Ru ; 8 in Na ; 9 and 10 in Co ; 11 in Fe ; 12 in Se. We shall return to these when analysing the elements, and shall meet many other proto-elemental groupings.

II.

The first thing which is noticed by the observer, when he turns his attention to the chemical atoms, is that they show certain definite forms, and that within these forms, modified in various ways, sub-groupings are observable which recur in connexion with the same modified form. The main types are not very numerous, and we found that, when we arranged the atoms we had observed, according to their external forms, they fell into natural classes ; when these, in turn, were compared with Sir William Crookes' classification, they proved to be singularly alike. Here is his arrangement of the elements, as it appeared in the Proceedings of the Royal Society, in a paper read on June 9th, 1898.*

* Our indebtedness to Sir William Crookes for his courtesy in lending us the above picture was acknowledged last month.

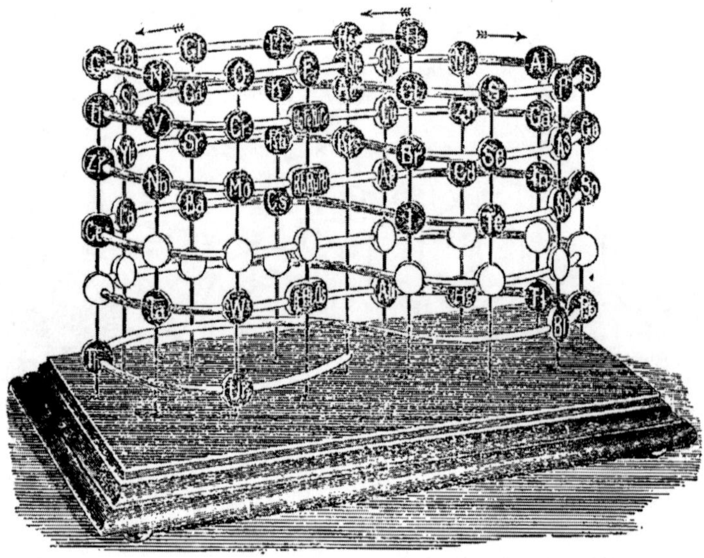

This is to be read, following the lines of the "figures of eight:" H, He, Li, Gl, B, C, N, and so on, each successive element being heavier than the one preceding it in order. The disks which fall immediately below each other form a class; thus: H, Cl, Br, I; these resemble each other in various ways, and, as we shall presently see, the same forms and groupings re-appear.

Another chart—taken from Erdmann's *Lehrbuch*—arranges the elements on a curved line, which curiously resembles the curves within the shell of a nautilus. The radiating lines show the classes, the whole diameter building up a family; it will be observed that there is an empty radius between hydrogen and helium, and we have placed occultum there; on the opposite radius, iron, rubidium and osmium are seen.

The external forms may be classified as follows; the internal details will be dealt with later:

I. *The dumb-bell.* The characteristics of this are a higher and lower group, each showing 12 projecting funnels, grouped round a central body, and a connecting rod. It appears in sodium, copper, silver, and gold, * and gold is given (1 on Plate III.), as the most extremely modified example of this form. The 12 almond-like

* The fifth member of this group was not sought for.

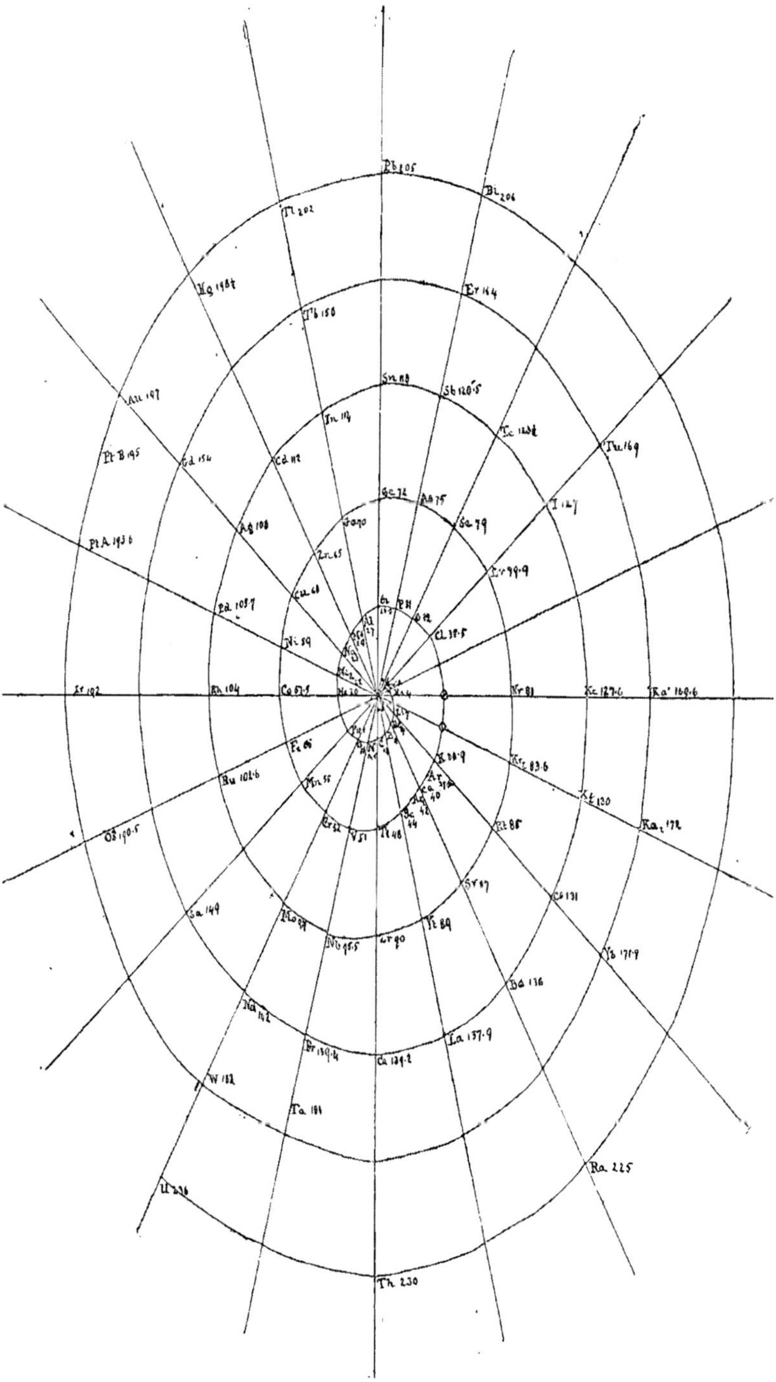

Pb 205
Bi 206
Tl 202
Hg 198.7
Er 164
Tb 150
Sn 118
Sb 120.5
In 114
Te 126.6
Tu 169
Au 197
Pt B 195
Gd 154
Cd 112
Ge 72
As 75
I 127
Ga 70
Se 79
Ag 108
Pt A 193.6
Zn 65
Br 79.9
Cu 63
P 31
Pd 106.7
Cl 35.5
Ni 59
Ir 192
Rh 104
Co 58.9
Kr 81
Xe 127.6
Ka' 169.6
Fe 56
Kr 83.6
K 38.9
Ru 101.6
Xe 130
Mn 55
Ka 172
Rb 85
Cr 52
V 51
Ti 48
Os 190.5
Sr 87
Cs 131
Sa 149
Mo 96
Yt 89
Nb 93.5
Zr 90
Yb 171.9
Ba 136
Nd 142
La 137.9
Pr 139.4
Ce 139.2
W 182
Ta 181
Ra 225
U 236
Th 230

Plate III.

1.

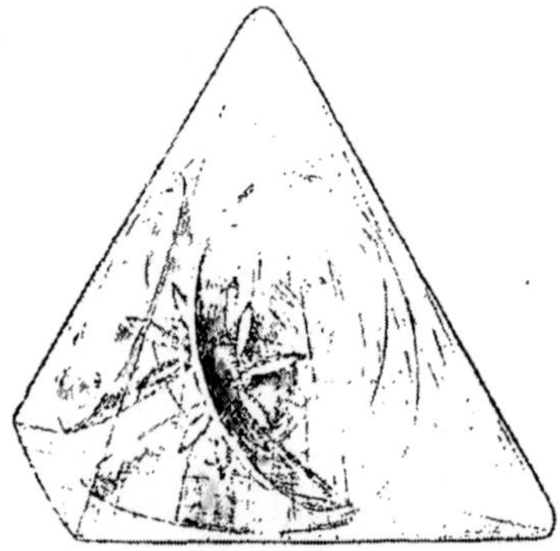

2.

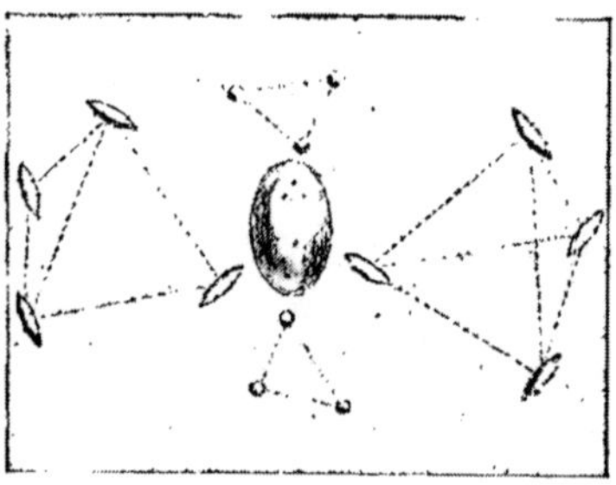

3.

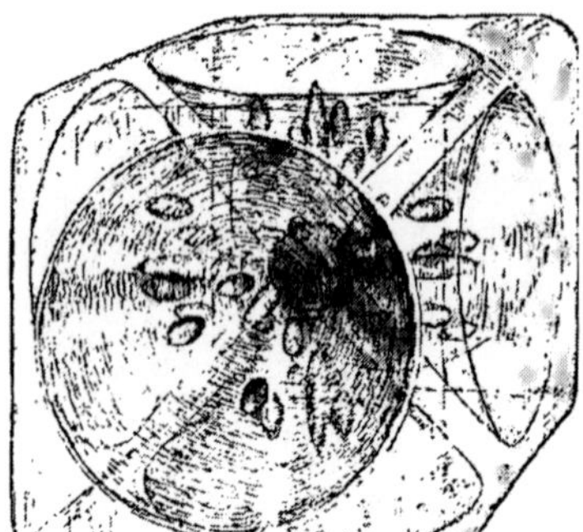

4.

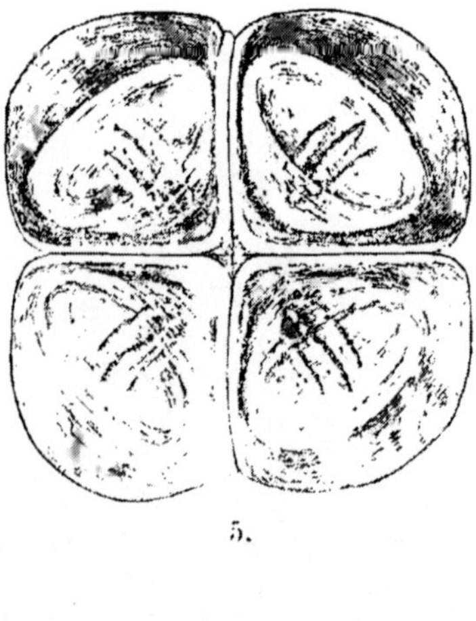

5.

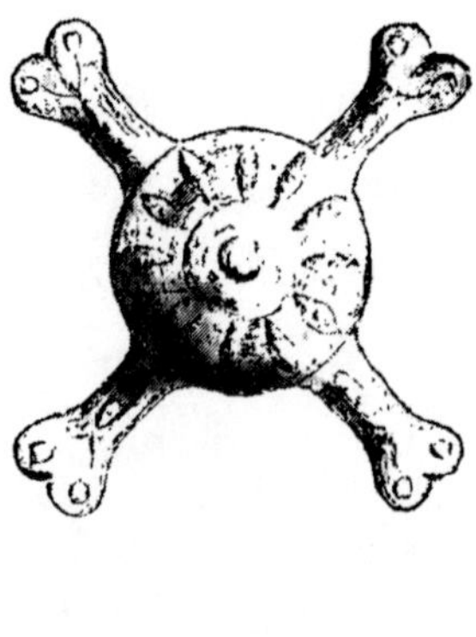

projections, above and below, are severally contained in shadowy funnels, impossible to reproduce in the drawing ; the central globe contains three globes, and the connecting portion has swollen out into an egg, with a very complicated central arrangement. The dumb-bell appears also in chlorine, bromine and iodine, but there is no trace of it in hydrogen, the head of the group. We have not met it elsewhere. It may be remarked that, in Sir William Crookes' scheme, in which they are all classed as monads, these two groups are the nearest to the neutral line, on the ingoing and outgoing series, and are respectively positive and negative.

II & II. *a. The tetrahedron.* The characteristics of this form are four funnels, containing ovoid bodies, opening on the face of a tetrahedron. The funnels generally, but not always, radiate from a central globe. We give beryllium (glucinum) as the simplest example (2 on Plate III.), and to this group belong calcium and strontium. The tetrahedron is the form of chromium and molybdenum, but not that of the head of their group, oxygen, which is, like hydrogen, *sui generis.* These two groups are marked in orthodox chemistry as respectively positive and negative, and are closely allied. Another pair of groups show the same tetrahedral form : magnesium, zinc and cadmium, positive ; sulphur, selenium and tellurium, negative. Selenium is a peculiarly beautiful element, with a star floating across the mouth of each funnel ; this star is extremely sensitive to light, and its rays tremble violently and bend if a beam of light falls on it. All these are duads.

The tetrahedron is not confined to the external form of the above atoms ; it seems to be one of the favorite forms of nature, and repeatedly appears in the internal arrangements. There is one tetrahedron within the unknown element occultum ; two appear in helium (3 on Plate III.) ; yttrium has also two within its cube, as has germanium ; five, intersecting, are found in neon, meta-neon, argon, metargon, krypton, meta-krypton, xenon, meta-xenon, kalon, meta-kalon, tin, titanium and zirconium. Gold contains no less than twenty tetrahedra.

III. *The cube.* The cube appears to be the form of triads. It has six funnels, containing ovoids, and opening on the faces of the cube. Boron is chosen as an example (4 on Plate III.). Its group members, scandium and yttrium have the same form; we have not examined the fourth; the group is positive. Its negative complement consists of nitrogen, vanadium and niobium, and we have again to note that nitrogen, like hydrogen and oxygen, departs from its group type. Two other triad groups, the positive aluminium, gallium and indium (the fourth unexamined) and the negative phosphorus, arsenic and antimony (the fourth unexamined), have also six funnels opening on the faces of a cube.

IV. *The Octahedron.* The simplest example of this is carbon (5 on Plate III.). We have again the funnel with its ovoids, but now there are eight funnels opening on the eight faces of the octahedron. In titanium (6 on Plate III.) the form is masked by the protruding arms, which give the appearance of the old Rosicrucian Cross and Rose, but when we look into the details later, the carbon type comes out clearly. Zirconium is exactly like titanium in form, but contains a larger number of atoms. We did not examine the remaining two members of this group. The group is tetratomic and positive. Its negative pendant shows the same form in silicon, germanium and tin; again, the fourth was unexamined.

V. *The Bars.* These characterise a set of closely allied groups, termed " inter-periodic." Fourteen bars (or seven crossed) radiate from a centre, as in iron (1 on Plate IV.), and the members of each group—iron, nickel, cobalt; ruthenium, rhodium, palladium; osmium, iridium, platinum—differ from each other by the weight of each bar, increasing in orderly succession; the details will be given later. Manganese is often grouped with iron, nickel, and cobalt (see Crookes' lemniscates), but its fourteen protruding bodies repeat the "lithium spike" (proto-element 5) and are grouped round a central ovoid. This would appear to connect it with lithium (2 on Plate IV.) rather than with fluorine (3 in Plate IV.), with which it is often classed. The " lithium spike" re-appears in potassium and rubidium. These details, again, will come out more clearly later

VI. *The Star.* A flat star, with five interpenetrating tetrahedra in the centre, is the characteristic of neon and its allies (4 on Plate IV.) leaving apart helium, which, as may be seen by referring to 3, Plate IV., has an entirely different form.

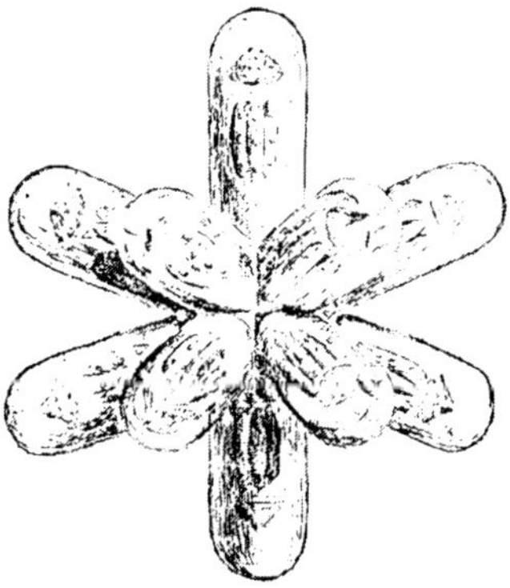

1.

2.

3.

4.

There are thus six clearly defined forms, typical of classes, with two—lithium and fluorine—of doubtful affinities. It is worthy of notice that in diatomic elements *four* funnels open on the faces of tetrahedra ; in triatomic, *six* funnels on the faces of cubes ; in tetratomic, *eight* funnels on the faces of octahedra. Thus we have a regular sequence of the platonic solids, and the question suggests itself, will further evolution develop elements shaped to the dodecahedron and the icosahedron ?

III.

We now pass from the consideration of the outer forms of the chemical elements to a study of their internal structure, the arrangement within the element of more or less complicated groups—proto-elements—capable of separate, independent, existence ; these are susceptible of further dissociation into simpler groups—meta-proto-elements—equally capable of separate, independent, existence ; these, once more, may be dissociated into yet simpler groups—hyper-meta-proto-elements—also capable of separate, independent existence, and resolvable into single ultimate physical atoms, the irreducible substratum of the physical world (see *ante*, pp. 354-356).

We shall have to study the general internal structure, and then the breaking up of each element, and the admirable diagrams, patiently worked out by Mr. Jinarâjadâsa, will make the study comparatively easy to carry on.

The diagrams, of course, can only give a very general idea of the facts they represent ; they give groupings and show relations, but much effort of the imagination is needed to transform the two-dimensional diagram into the three-dimensional object. The wise student will try to visualise the figure from the diagram. Thus the two triangles of hydrogen are not in one plane ; the circles are spheres, and the atoms within them, while preserving to each other their relative positions, are in swift movement in three-dimensional space. Where five atoms are seen, as in bromine and iodine, they are generally arranged with the central atom above the four, and their motion indicates lines which erect four plane triangles—meeting at their apices—on a square base, forming a square-based four-sided pyramid. Each dot represents a single ultimate atom. The enclosing lines indicate the impression of form made on the observer, and the groupings of the atoms; the groups will divide along these lines, when the element is broken up, so that the lines have significance, but they do not exist as stable walls or enclosing films, but rather mark limits, not lines, of vibrations. It should be noted that it is not possible to show five of the prisms in the five intersecting tetrahedra of prisms, and 30 atoms must, therefore, be added in counting.

The diagrams are not drawn to scale, as such drawing would be impossible; the dot representing the atom is enormously too large compared with the enclosures, which are absurdly too small; a scale drawing would mean an almost invisible dot on a sheet of many yards square.

The use of the words 'positive' and 'negative' needs to be guarded by the following paragraphs from the article on 'Chemistry' in the *Encyclopædia Britannica*. We use the words in their ordinary text-book meaning, and have not, so far, detected any characteristics whereby an element can be declared, at sight, to be either positive or negative:

"When binary compounds, or compounds of two elements, are decomposed by an electric current, the two elements make their appearance at opposite poles. Those elements which are disengaged at the negative pole are termed electro-positive or positive or basylous elements, while those disengaged at the positive pole are termed electro-negative or negative or chlorous elements. But the difference between these two classes of elements is one of degree only, and they gradually merge into each other; moreover the electric relations of elements are not absolute, but vary according to the state of combination in which they exist, so that it is just as impossible to divide the elements into two classes according to this property as it is to separate them into two distinct classes of metals and non-metals."

We follow here the grouping according to external forms, and the student should compare it with the groups marked in the lemniscate arrangement shown in Article II.(p. 377, properly p. 437, February), reading the group by the disks that fall below each other; thus the first group is H, Cl, Br, I, (hydrogen, chlorine, bromine, iodine) and a blank for an undiscovered element. The elements grow denser in descending order; thus hydrogen is an invisible gas; chlorine a denser gas visible by its color; bromine is a liquid; iodine is a solid—all, of course, when temperature and pressure are normal. By the lowering of temperature and the increase of pressure, an element which is normally gaseous becomes a liquid, and then a solid. Solid, liquid, gaseous, are three interchangeable states of matter, and an element does not alter its constitution by changing its state. So far as a chemical 'atom' is concerned, it matters not whether it be drawn for investigation from a solid, a liquid, or a gas; but the internal arrangements of the 'atoms' become much more complicated as they become denser and denser, as is seen by the complex arrangements necessitated by the presence of the 3546 ultimate atoms contained in the chemical 'atom' of gold, as compared with the simple arrangement of the 18 ultimate atoms of hydrogen.

According to the lemniscate arrangement, we should commence with hydrogen as the head of the first negative group, but as it differs wholly from those placed with it, it is better to take it by itself. Hydrogen is the lightest of the known elements, and is therefore taken as 1 in ordinary chemistry, and all atomic weights are multiples of this. We take it as 18, because it contains eighteen ultimate atoms, the smallest number we have found in a chemical element. So our 'number weights' are obtained by dividing the total number of atoms in an element by 18 (see p. 349, January).

HYDROGEN (Plate V., 1). Hydrogen not only stands apart from its reputed group by not having the characteristic dumb-bell shape, well shown in sodium (Plate I opposite p. 349, January), but it also stands apart in being positive, serving as a base, not as a chlorous, or acid, radical, thus "playing the part of a metal," as in hydrogen chloride (hydrochloric acid), hydrogen sulphate (sulphuric acid), etc.

It is most curious that hydrogen, oxygen and nitrogen, the most widely spread gases, all differ fundamentally in form from the groups they reputedly head.* Hydrogen was the first chemical

* Since writing the above, I have noticed, in the *London Edinburgh and Dublin Philosophical Magazine and Journal of Science*, conducted by Dr. John Joly and Mr. William Francis, in an article entitled "Evolution and Devolution of the Elements," the statement that it is probable that in "the nebulous state of matter there are four substances, the first two being unknown upon earth, the third being hydrogen and the fourth . . . . helium. It also seems probable that

element examined by us, nearly thirteen years ago, and I reproduce here the substance of what I wrote in November, 1895, for we have nothing to add to nor amend in it.

PLATE V.

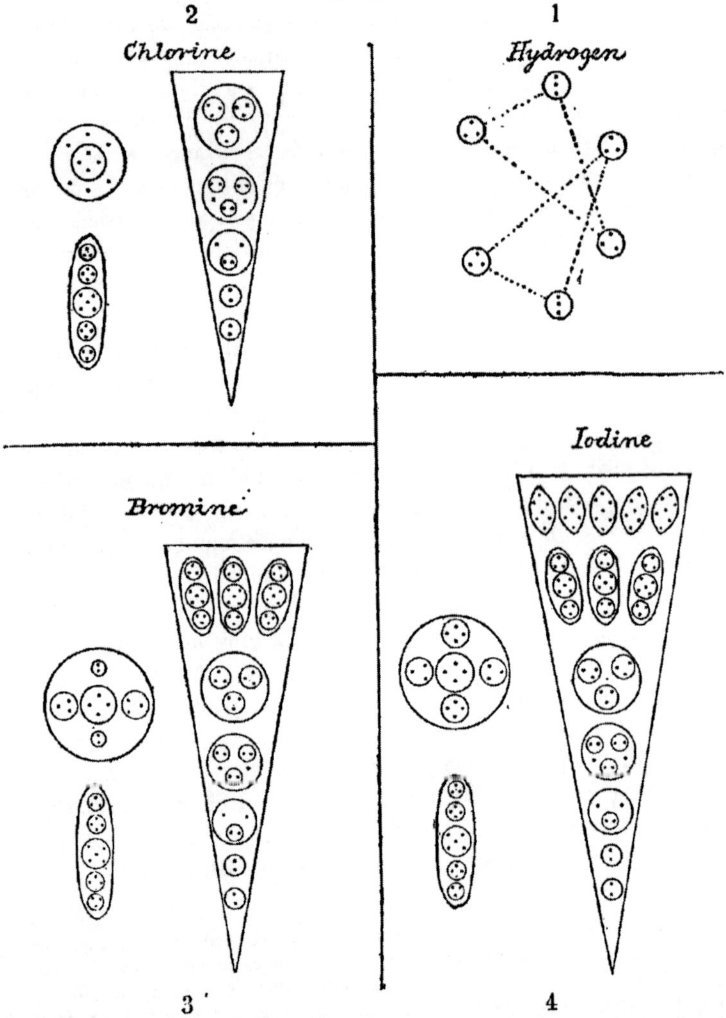

. . . . hydrogen, the two unknown elements, and helium are the four original elements from which all the other elements form. To distinguish them from the others we will term them protons." This is suggestive as regards hydrogen, but does not help us with regard to oxygen and nitrogen.

Hydrogen consists of six small bodies, contained in an egg-like form (the outer forms are not given in the diagrams). The six little bodies are arranged in two sets of three, forming two triangles which are not interchangeable, but are related to each other as object and image. The six bodies are not all alike; they each contain three ultimate physical atoms, but in four of the bodies the three atoms are arranged in a triangle, and in the remaining two in a line.

HYDROGEN :	6 bodies of 3	...	18
	Atomic Weight	...	1
	Number Weight $\frac{18}{18}$	...	1

I. THE DUMB-BELL GROUP.

1*a*. This group consists of Cl, Br, and I, (chlorine, bromine and iodine); they are monads, diamagnetic and negative.

CHLORINE (Plate V., 2).—As already said, the general form is that of the dumb-bell, the lower and upper parts each consisting of twelve funnels, six sloping upwards and six downwards, the funnels radiating outwards from a central globe, and these two parts being united by a connecting rod (see, again, sodium, Plate I).

The funnel (shown flat as an isosceles triangle, standing on its apex) is a somewhat complicated structure, of the same type as that in sodium (Plate VI., 2), the difference consisting in the addition of one more globe, containing nine additional atoms. The central globe is the same as in sodium, but the connecting rod differs. We have here a regular arrangement of five globes, containing three, four, five, four, three atoms respectively, whereas sodium has only three bodies, containing four, six, four. But copper and silver, its congeners, have their connecting rods of exactly the same pattern as the chlorine rod, and the chlorine rod reappears in both bromine and iodine. These close similarities point to some real relation between these groups of elements, which are placed, in the lemniscates, equi-distant from the central line, though one is on the swing which is going towards that line and the other is on the swing away from it.

CHLORINE :	Upper Part { 12 funnels of 25 atoms	...	300
	{ Central Globe	...	10
	Lower Part Same	...	310
	Connecting Rod	...	19
		Total ...	639

Atomic Weight	...	35·473
Number Weight $\frac{639}{18}$	...	35·50

(The Atomic Weights are mostly from Erdmann, and the Number Weights are those ascertained by us by counting the atoms as described on p. 349, January, and dividing by 18. Prof. T. W. Richards, in *Nature*, July 18, 1907, gives 35·473.)

BROMINE (Plate V., 3).—In bromine, each funnel has three additional bodies, ovoid in shape, an addition of 33 atoms being thus made without any disturbance of form; two pairs of atoms are added to the central globe, and a rearrangement of the atoms is effected by drawing together and lessening the swing of the pair of triplets, thus making symmetrical room for the new-comers. The connecting rod remains unchanged. The total number of atoms is thus raised from the 639 of chlorine to 1439. Over and over again, in these investigations, were we reminded of Tyndall's fascinating description of crystal building, and his fancy of the tiny, ingenious builders busied therein. Truly are there such builders, and the ingenuity and effectiveness of their devices are delightful to see.*

BROMINE :	Upper Part	12 funnels of 58 atoms	...	696
		Central Globe	...	14
	Lower Part Same		...	710
	Connecting Rod		...	19
			Total ...	1439
	Atomic Weight		...	79·953
	Number Weight $\frac{1439}{18}$		...	79·944

IODINE (Plate V., 4).—We find herein that the central globe gains 4 atoms, the two pairs becoming 2 quartets; the connecting rod exactly reproduces the rods of chlorine and bromine; the funnel is also that of bromine, except that five bodies, containing 35 atoms, are added to it. The 1439 atoms of bromine are thus raised to 2887.

IODINE :	Upper Part	12 funnels of 93 atoms	...	1116
		Central Globe	...	18
	Lower Part Same		...	1134
	Connecting Rod		...	19
			Total ...	2287
	Atomic Weight		...	126·01
	Number Weight $\frac{2287}{18}$		...	127·055

* Theosophists call them Nature-Spirits, and often use the mediæval term Elementals. Beings concerned with the elements truly are they, even with chemical elements.

The plan underlying the building up of groups is here clearly shown ; a figure is built up on a certain plan, in this case a dumb-bell ; in the succeeding members of the group additional atoms are symmetrically introduced, modifying the appearance, but following the general idea ; in this case the connecting rod remains unaltered, while the two ends become larger and larger, more and more

PLATE VI.

2 1

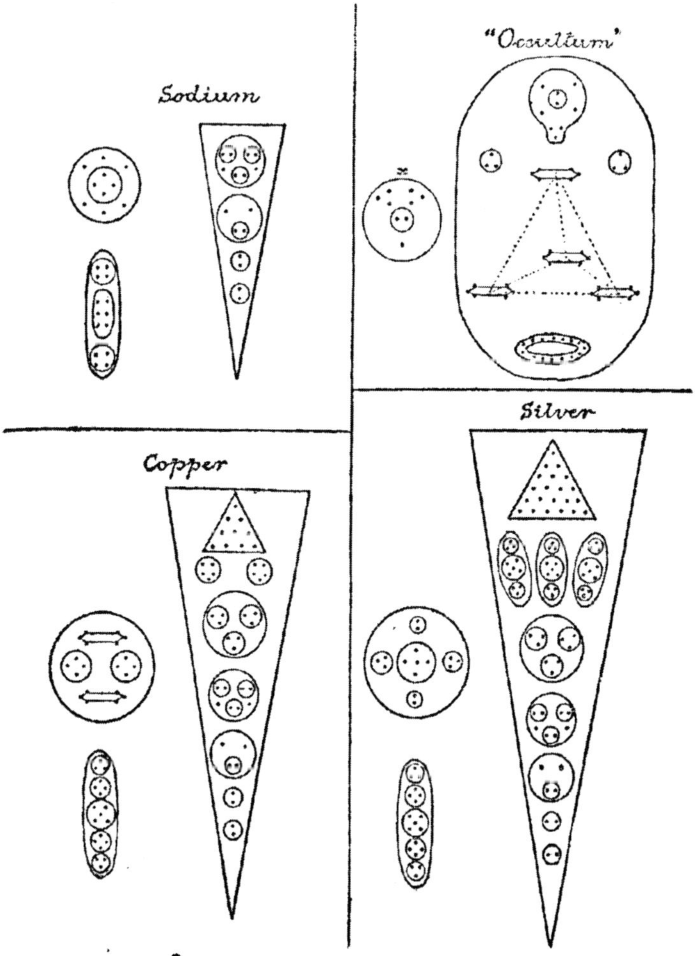

3 4

overshadowing it, and causing it to become shorter and thicker. Thus a group is gradually formed by additional symmetrical additions. In the undiscovered remaining member of the group we may suppose that the rod will have become still more egg-like, as in the case of gold.

I (*b*). The corresponding positive group to that which we have been considering consists of Na, Cu, Ag, and Au (sodium, copper, silver and gold), with an empty disk between silver and gold, showing where an element ought to be. These four elements are monads, diamagnetic, and positive, and they show the dumb-bell arrangement, although it is much modified in gold ; we may presume that the undiscovered element between silver and gold would form a link between them.

SODIUM (Plate VI., 2) has been already described (p. 349, January), as a type of the group, so we need only refer to its internal arrangement in order to note that it is the simplest of the dumb-bell group. Its twelve funnels show only four enclosed bodies, the same as we see in chlorine, bromine, iodine, copper and silver, and which is very little modified in gold. Its central globe is the simplest of all, as is its connecting rod. We may therefore take it that sodium is the ground-plan of the whole group.

SODIUM :	Upper Part	12 funnels of 16 each ...	192
		Central Globe ...	10
	Lower Part	Same ...	202
	Connecting Rod	...	14
		Total ...	418
	Atomic Weight	...	23·88
	Number Weight $\frac{418}{18}$	...	23·22

COPPER (Plate VI., 3) introduces an addition in the funnel, that we shall find elsewhere, *e.g.*, in silver, gold, iron, platinum, zinc, tin, the triangular arrangement near the mouth of the funnel and adds to the ten atoms in this nineteen more in three additional enclosed bodies, thus raising the number of atoms in a funnel from the sixteen of sodium to forty-five. The number in the central globe is doubled, and we meet for the first time the peculiar cigar or prism-shaped six-atomed arrangement, that is one of the most common of atomic groups. It ought to imply some definite quality, with its continual recurrence. The central column is the three, four, five, four, three, arrangement already noted.

COPPER :	Upper Part	12 funnels of 45 atoms ...	540
		Central Globe ...	20
	Lower Part	Same ...	560
	Connecting Rod	...	19
		Total ...	1139
	Atomic Weight	...	63·12
	Number Weight $\frac{1139}{18}$	...	63·277

SILVER (Plate VI., 4) follows copper in the constitution of five of the bodies enclosed in the funnels. But the triangular group contains twenty-one atoms as against ten, and three ovoids, each containing three bodies with eleven atoms, raise the number of atoms in a funnel to seventy-nine. The central globe is decreased by five, and the prisms have disappeared. The connecting rod is unaltered.

SILVER :	Upper Part	12 funnels of 79 atoms ...	489
		Central Globe ...	15
	Lower Part	Same ...	963
	Connecting Rod	...	19
		Total ...	1945
	Atomic Weight		107·93
	Number Weight $\frac{1945}{18}$		108·055

(This atomic weight is given by Stas, in *Nature*, August 29, 1907, but it has been argued later that the weight should not be above 107·883.)

GOLD (Plate VII.) is so complicated that it demands a whole plate to itself. It is difficult to recognise the familiar dumb-bell in this elongated egg, but when we come to examine it, the characteristic groupings appear. The egg is the enormously swollen connecting rod, and the upper and lower parts with their central globes are the almond-like projections above and below, with the central ovoid. Round each almond is a shadowy funnel (not drawn in the diagram), and within the almond is the collection of bodies shown in *e*, wherein the two

PLATE VII.

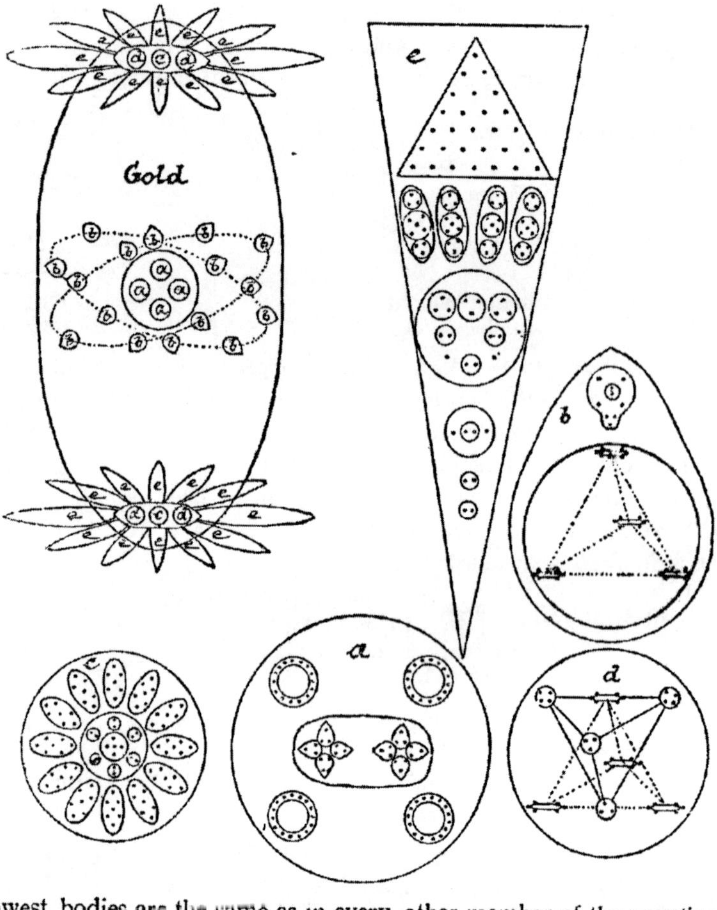

lowest bodies are the same as in every other member of the negative and positive groups ; the third, ascending, is a very slight modification of the other thirds ; the fourth is a union and re-arrangement of the fourth and fifth ; the fifth, of four ovoids, adds one to the three ovoids of bromine, iodine and silver ; the triangular group is like that in copper and silver, though with 28 atoms instead of 10 or 21, and it may be noted that the cone in iron has also 28. The central body in the ovoid is very complicated, and is shown in *c*. The bodies on each side, *d*, are each made up of two tetrahedra, one with four six-atomed prisms at its angles, and the other with four spheres, a pair with four atoms and a pair with three. We then come to the connecting rod. One of the four similar groups in the centre is enlarged in *a*, and one of the sixteen circling groups is enlarged in *b*. These groups are arranged in two planes inclined to one another.

GOLD:	Upper Part	12 funnels of 97 atoms	...	1164
		Central ovoid *c*	...	101
		2 *d*, 38	...	76
	Lower Part	Same	...	1341
	Connecting Rod	4 *a* 84	...	336
		16 *b* 33	...	528
			Total ...	3546
	Atomic Weight		...	195·74
	Number Weight $\frac{3546}{18}$		...	197

It may be noted that the connecting rod is made up of exactly sixteen atoms of occultum, and that sixteen such atoms contain 864 ultimate atoms, the exact member of atoms in titanium.

IV.

Occultum was observed by us in 1895, and, finding that it was so light, and so simple in its composition, we thought that it might be helium, of which we were unable, at the time, to obtain a sample. When, however, helium itself came under observation in 1907, it proved to be quite different from the object before observed, so we dubbed the unrecognised object Occultum, until orthodox science shall find it and label it in proper fashion.

OCCULTUM (Plate VI., 1, p. 21).

We here meet the tetrahedron for the first time, with each angle occupied by a six-atomed group, the atoms arranged as on the end triangles of a prism. This form recurs very often, and was noted, last month, as seen in copper (Plate VI., 3); it revolves with extreme rapidity around its longitudinal axis, and looks like a pencil sharpened at both ends, or a cigar tapering at both ends; we habitually spoke of it as 'the cigar.' It appears to be strongly coherent, for, as will be seen below, its six atoms remain attached to each other as meta-compounds, and even when divided into two triplets as hyper-compounds, they revolve round each other.

Above the tetrahedron is a balloon-shaped figure, apparently drawn into shape by the attraction of the tetrahedron. The body below the tetrahedron looks like a coil of rope, and contains fifteen atoms ; they are arranged on a slanting disk in a flat ring, and the force goes in at the top of one atom, and out of the bottom of it into the top of the next, and so on, making a closed circuit. The two little spheres, each containing a triplet, are like fill-up paragraphs to a compositor—they seem to be kept standing, and popped in where wanted. The sphere marked x is a proto-compound, the balloon when set free.

As was noted under gold (p. 25), sixteen occultum bodies, re-arranged, make up the connecting rod in gold :—

OCCULTUM :	Tetrahedron	... 24
	Balloon	... 9
	Triplets	... 6
	Rope-Circle	... 15
	Total	... 54

Atomic Weight	Not known
Number Weight $\frac{54}{18}$	... 3

DISSOCIATION OF ATOMS.

Before proceeding to the study of other chemical atoms, as to their general internal arrangements, it is desirable to follow out, in those already shown, the way in which these atoms break up into simpler forms, yielding successively what we have called proto, meta, and hyper-compounds. It is naturally easier to follow these in the simpler atoms than in the more complex, and if the earlier dissociations are shown, the latter can be more readily and more intelligibly described.

The first thing that happens on removing a gaseous atom from its 'hole' (see pp. 5—7) or encircling 'wall,' is that the contained bodies are set free, and, evidently released from tremendous pressure, assume spherical or ovoid forms, the atoms within each re-arranging themselves, more or less, within the new 'hole' or 'wall.' The figures are, of course, three-dimensional, and often remind one of crystals ; tetrahedral, octagonal, and other like forms being of constant occurrence. In the diagrams of the proto-compounds, the constituent atoms are shown by dots. In the diagrams of the meta-compounds the dot becomes a heart, in order to show the resultants of the lines of force. In the diagrams of the hyper-compounds the same plan is followed. The letters *a*, *b*, *c*, etc., enable the student to follow the breaking up of each group through its successive stages.

HYDROGEN (Plate V., 1, p. 18).

The six bodies contained in the gaseous atom instantaneously re-arrange themselves within two spheres ; the two linear triplets unite with one triangular triplet, holding to each other relative positions which, if connected by three right lines, would form a triangle with a triplet at each angle ; the remaining three triangular triplets

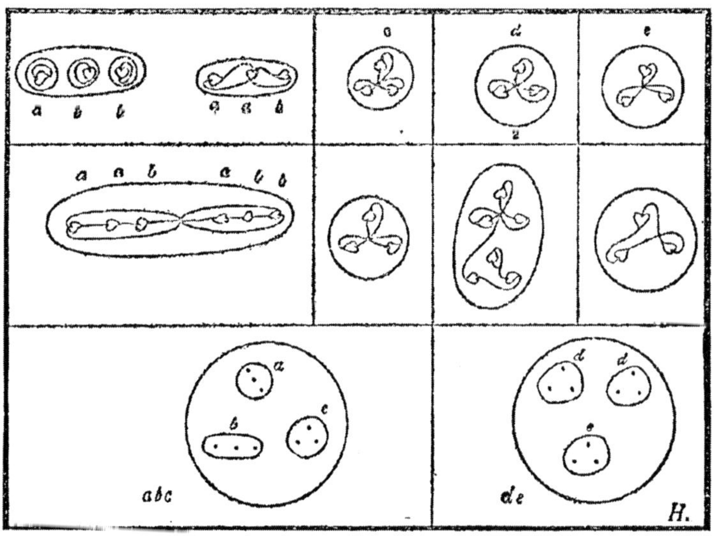

similarly arrange themselves in the second sphere. These form the proto-compounds of hydrogen.

In the dissociation of these, each group breaks up into two, the two linear triplets joining each other and setting free their triangular comrade, while two of the triangular triplets similarly remain together, casting out the third, so that hydrogen yields four meta-compounds.

In the hyper-condition, the connexion between the double triplets is broken, and they become four independent groups, two like ix, in the hyper-types (p. 9), and two remaining linear, but re-arranging their internal relations; the two remaining groups break up into two pairs and a unit.

The final dissociation sets all the atoms free.

OCCULTUM (Plate VI., 1, p. 21).

On the first dissociation of the component parts of helium, the tetrahedron separates as a whole, with its four 'cigars,' flattening itself out within its hole, *a*; two 'cigars' are positive and two negative, marked respectively *a* and *a'*. The rope becomes a ring within a sphere, *b*, and the two bodies *d*, *d*, which are loose in the gaseous atom, come within this ring. The balloon becomes a sphere.

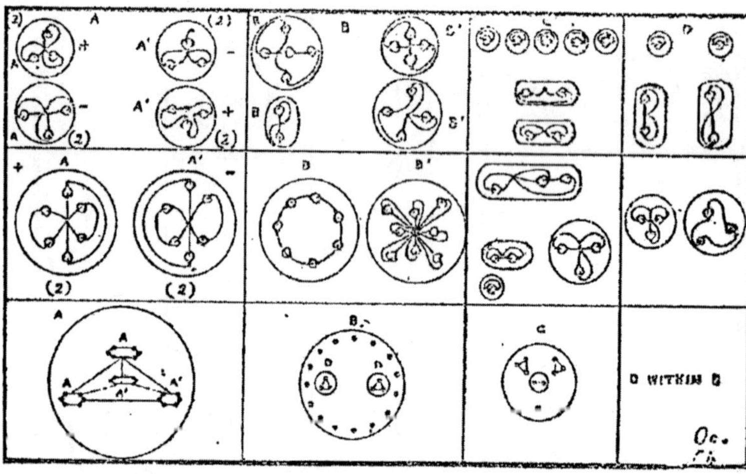

On further dissociation, the 'cigars' go off independently, showing two types, and these again each divide into triplets, as meta-compounds. *B*, on the meta-level, casts out the two *d* bodies, which become independent triplets, and the 'rope' breaks into two, a close ring of seven atoms and a double cross of eight. These subdivide again to form hyper-compounds, the ring yielding a quintet and a pair, and the double cross separating into its two parts.

The balloon, *c*, becomes much divided, the cohesion of its parts being slight; it forms two triplets, a pair and a unit, and these set free, on further dissociation, no less than five separate atoms and two duads.

The two triplets of *d* each cast out an atom on dissociation, and form two pairs and two units.

SODIUM (Plate VI., 2).

It is convenient to consider sodium next, because it is the basic pattern on which not only copper, silver and gold are formed, but also chlorine, bromine and iodine.

When sodium is set free from its gaseous condition, it divides up into thirty-one bodies—twenty-four separate funnels, four bodies derived from the two central globes, and three from the connecting rod. The funnels become spheres, and each contains four enclosed spheres, with more or less complicated contents. Each central globe yields a sextet and a quartet, and the rod sets free two quartets and a peculiarly formed sextet.

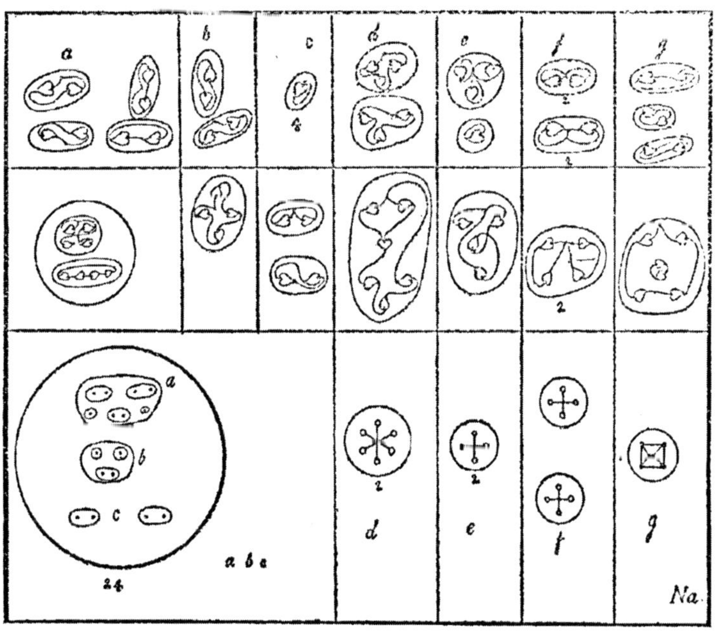

When the proto-compounds are dissociated, the funnel-sphere sets free : (1) the contents of *a*, rearranged into two groups of four within a common sphere ; the sphere yields four duads as hyper-compounds ; (2) the contents of *b*, which unite themselves into a quartet, yielding two duads as hyper-compounds ; and (3) the contents of the two spheres, *c*, which maintain their separation as meta-compounds, and become entirely independent, the atoms within the sphere revolving round each other, but the spheres ceasing their revolution round a common axis, and going off in different directions. The atoms break off from each other, and gyrate in independent solitude as hyper-' compounds.' Thus each funnel yields finally ten hyper-bodies.

The part of the central globe, marked *d*, with its six atoms, whirling round a common centre, becomes two triplets, at the meta-stage, preparing for the complete separation of these as hyper-bodies. The second part of the same globe, marked *e*, a whirling cross, with an atom at each point, becomes a quartet in the meta-state, in which three atoms revolve round a fourth, and in the hyper-state, this central atom is set free, leaving a triplet and a unit.

Each of the two bodies marked *f*, liberated from the connecting rod, shows four atoms whirling round a common centre, exactly resembling *e* in appearance ; but there must be some difference of inner relations, for, in the meta-state, they re-arrange themselves as two pairs, and divide into two as hyper-bodies.

The body marked *g* is a four-sided pyramid, with two closely joined atoms at its apex ; these still cling to each in mutual revolution as a meta-body, encircled by a ring of four, and this leads to the further dissociation into three pairs on the hyper-level.

CHLORINE (Plate V., 2, p. 18).

The description of the funnel of sodium applies to that of chlorine, until we come to the body nearest the mouth, the sphere containing three additional bodies ; this remains within the funnel in the first dissociation, so that again we have twenty-four separate funnels as proto-compounds ; the central globes are the same as in sodium, and yield the same four bodies ; the connecting rod sets free five bodies, of which two are the same ; we have thus thirty-three separate bodies as the result of the dissociation of chlorine into its proto compounds. As all the compounds which are in sodium break up in the same way into meta and hyper-co'npounds, we need not repeat the process here. We have only to consider the new meta and hyper-compounds of the highest sphere within the funnel, and the two triplets and one quintet from the connecting iod.

The additional body within the proto-funnel is of a very simple character, three contained triangles within the flattened sphere. On release from the funnel, on the meta-level, the atoms re-arrange themselves in a whirling set of three triplets, and these break off from each other as hyper-compounds. The two triplets from the connecting rod, also, are of the simplest character and need not delay us. The five-atomed body, a four-sided pyramid as a proto-compound, becomes a ring whirling round a centre on the meta, and two pairs with a unit on the hyper.

Bromine (Plate V., 3).

Three additional bodies appear at the top of the funnel, which otherwise repeats that of chlorine. The connecting rod is the same and may be disregarded. The central globes become nioie complex.

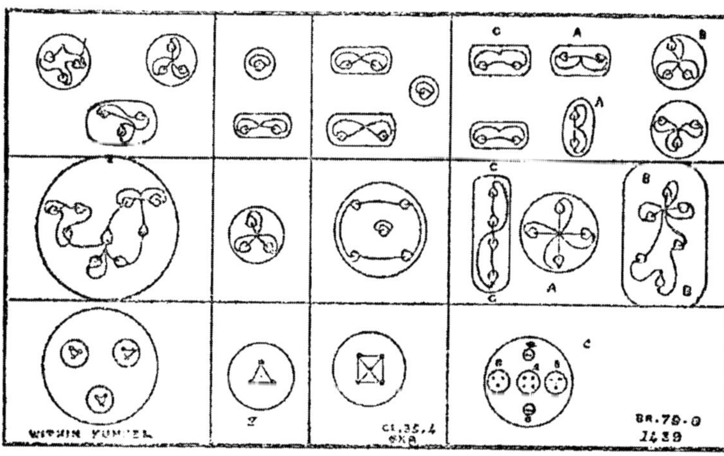

The additions are, however, of very easy types, and hence are readily dealt with. Each of the three similar ovoid bodies contains two triplets—each a triangle and a quintet—a four-sided pyramid,

These are the same, as may be seen in the connecting rod of chlorine, and we need not repeat them. Only the globe remains. This does not break up as a proto-compound but is merely set free, *a* and the 2 *bs* whirling in a plane vertical to the paper and the two smaller bodies, *cc*, whirling on a plane at right angles to the other. These two disengage themselves, forming a quartet as a meta-compound, while *a* makes a whirling cross and *bb* a single sextet; these further dissociate themselves into four pairs and two triplets.

IODINE (Plate V., 4).

Iodine has nothing new to give us, except five similar ovoid bodies at the top of each funnel, and two quartets instead of two pairs in the central globe. The ovoid bodies become spheres when the funnels are thrown off, and a crystalline form is indicated within the sphere. The atoms are arranged in two tetrahedra with a common apex, and the relationship is maintained in the meta-body, a septet. The latter breaks up into two triplets and a unit on the hyper-level. In the central globes, the *a* of bromine is repeated twice instead of the pairs in *cc*.

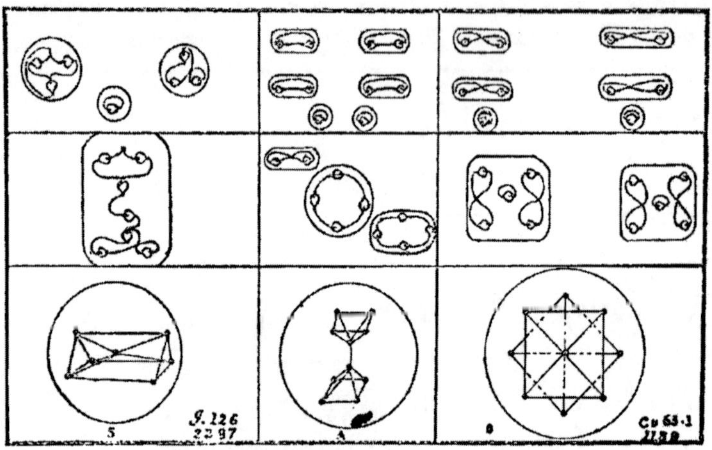

COPPER (Plate VI., 3).

We have already disposed of occultum, on this plate, and of sodium, which lies at the root of both groups. Copper, we now find, is also very largely off our hands, as the funnel provides us with only two new types—two spheres—each containing five atoms in a new arrangement, and the triangular body at the mouth with its ten atoms. This triangular body, with an increased number of atoms, re-appears in various other chemical elements. The central globes are different from any we have had before, in their internal arrangement, but the constituents are familiar; there are two contained spheres with four atoms each, the *a* in the globe of bromine (see above) and 2 'cigars.' The 'cigars' may be followed under occultum, (see above). The connecting rod is as in chlorine, bromine and iodine.

The atoms in the bodies *a* and *b* are curiously arranged. *A* consists of two square-based pyramids turned so as meet at their apices, and breaks up into two quartet rings and a duad. *B* is again two four-sided pyramids, but the bases are in contact and set at right angles to each other; the second apex is not seen, as it is directly below the first. The pyramids separate as meta-bodies, and the atoms assume the peculiar arrangement indicated and then break up into four pairs and two units on the hyper level.

V.

SILVER (PLATE VI., 4 and Ag. below).

Silver presents us with only two new bodies, and even these are only new by slight additions to old models. The triangular-shaped body at the apex of the funnel, containing 21 atoms, is intermediate between the similar bodies in copper and iron. As a proto-element it becomes three triangles, joined at their apices, in fact a tetrahedron in which no atoms are distributed on the fourth face. The faces separate on the meta level and give three seven-atomed figures, and each of these breaks up into two triplets and a unit. The central globe only differs from that of bromine by the addition of one atom, which gives the familiar four-sided pyramid with a square base as in chlorine (see p. 31).

GOLD (PLATE VII and Au. below).

The disintegration of gold first yields forty-seven bodies on the proto-level; the twenty-four funnels separate, and the central globes which hold each twelve together set free their six contained globes (*c*, *d*), thirty bodies being thus liberated. The sixteen bodies on the central inclined planes, marked *b*, break away, their central globe,

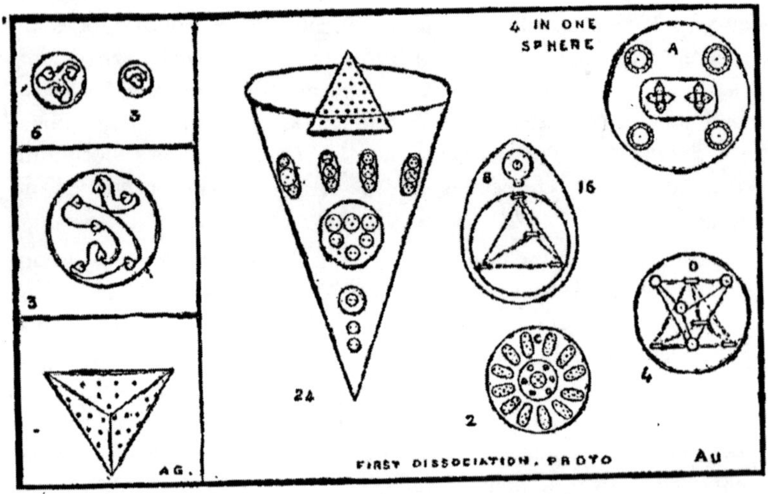

with its four contained globes, remaining unchanged. But this condition does not last. The motion of the funnels changes and thus the funnels cease to exist and their contents are set free, each funnel thus liberating nine independent bodies; the sixteen *b* separate into two each; the four *a* liberate five each; the two *c* set free thirteen each; the four *d*, finally liberate two each: 302 proto elements in all.

The funnel is almost that of iodine, re-arranged. Four of the first ring in the iodine funnel are replaced by the triangular body, which becomes a four-sided pyramid with an occupied base. The second ring of three ovoids in iodine becomes four in gold, but the internal arrangement of each ovoid is the same. The next two spheres in the iodine funnel coalesce into one sphere, with similar contents, in the gold funnel. The fifth in iodine is slightly re-arranged to form the fourth in descent in gold, and the remaining two are the same. *B* has been broken up under occultum (p. 628) and can be followed there. The sixteen rings set free from the four *a*, after gyrating round the central body, now become a sphere, break up, as in occultum (see p. 28) into a meta seven-atomed ring and an eight-atomed double cross, and so on to the hyper level. The sphere with its two contained bodies breaks up into eight triangles on the meta level, and each of these, on the hyper, into a duad and a unit. The twelve septets of *c* assume the form of prisms as in iodine (see p. 32) and pursue the same course, while its central body, a four-sided pyramid with its six attendants, divides on the meta level into six duads, revolving round a ring with a central atom as in chlorine (p. 31), the duads going off independently on the hyper-level and the ring breaking up as in chlorine. The 'cigar' tetrahedron of *d* follows its course as in occultum, and the other sets free two quartets and two triplets on the meta level, yielding six duads and two units as hyper compounds. It will be seen that, complex as gold is, it is composed of constituents already familiar, and has iodine and occultum as its nearest allies.

II AND II*a*.—THE TETRAHEDRAL GROUPS.

II. This group consists of beryllium (glucinum), calcium, strontium and barium, all diatomic, paramagnetic and positive. The corresponding group consists of oxygen, chromium, molybdenum, wolfram (tungstan) and uranium, with a blank disk between wolfram and uranium : these are diatomic, paramagnetic, and negative. We have not examined barium, wolfram, or uranium.

BERYLLIUM Plate III. 2 and Plate VIII. 1). In the tetrahedron four funnels are found, the mouth of each funnel opening on one of its faces. The funnels radiate from a central globe, and each funnel contains four ovoids each with ten atoms within it arranged in three spheres. In the accompanying diagrams one funnel with its four ovoids is shown and a single ovoid with its three spheres, containing severally three, four, and three atoms, is seen at the left-hand corner of the plate (7 *a*). The members of this group are alike in arrangement, differing only in the increased complexity of the bodies contained in the funnels. Beryllium, it will be observed, is very simple, whereas calcium and strontium are complicated.

BERYLLIUM : 4 funnels of 40 atoms	...	160
Central globe	...	4
Total	...	164
Atomic weight	...	9·01
Number weight $\frac{164}{18}$	...	9·11

PLATE VIII.

CALCIUM (Plate VIII., 2) shows in each funnel three contained spheres, of which the central one has within it seven ovoids identical with those of beryllium, and the spheres above and below it contain

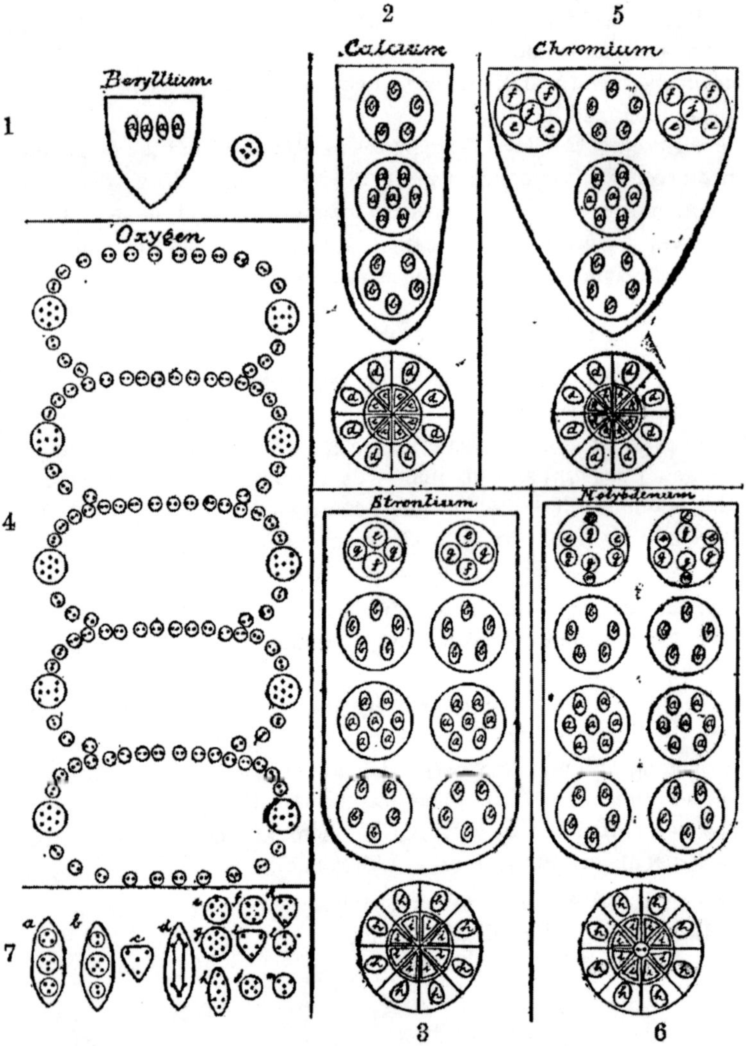

each five ovoids (7 *b*) in which the three contained spheres have, respectively, two, five, and two atoms. The central globe is double, globe within globe, and is divided into eight segments, radiating from the centre like an orange ; the internal part of the segment belonging to the inner globe has a triangular body within it, containing four atoms (7 *c*), and the external part, belonging to the encircling globe, shows the familiar ' cigar ' (7 *d*). In this way 720 atoms are packed into the simple beryllium type.

CALCIUM : 4 funnels of 160 atoms	...	640
Central globe	...	80
Total	...	720
Atomic weight	...	39·74
Number weight $\frac{720}{18}$	..	40·00

STRONTIUM (Plate VIII., 3) shows a still further complication within the funnels, no less than eight spheres being found within each. Each of the highest pair contains four subsidiary spheres, with five, seven, seven, five atoms, respectively (7 *e*, *g*, *f*). The *g* groups are identical with those in gold, but difference of pressure makes the containing body spherical instead of ovoid ; similar groups are seen in the top ring of the iodine funnel, where also the ' hole ' is ovoid in form. The second pair of spheres contains ten ovoids (7 *b*) identical with those of calcium. The third pair contains fourteen ovoids (7 *a*) identical with those of beryllium, while the fourth pair repeats the second, with the ovoids re-arranged. The internal divisions of the double sphere of the central globe are the same as in calcium, but the contents differ. The ' cigars ' in the external segments are replaced by seven-atomed ovoids (7 *h*)—the iodine ovoids—and the external segments contain five-atomed triangles (7 *i*). Thus 1568 atoms have been packed into the beryllium type, and our wonder is again aroused by the ingenuity with which a type is preserved while it is adapted to new conditions.

STRONTIUM : 4 funnels of 368 atoms	...	1472
Central globe	...	96
Total	...	1568
Atomic weight	...	86·95
Number weight $\frac{1568}{18}$	...	87·11

The corresponding group, headed by oxygen—oxygen, chromium, molybdenum, wolfram and uranium—offers us another problem in its first member.

OXYGEN (Plate VIII., 4). This was examined by us in 1895, and the description may be reproduced here with a much improved diagram of its very peculiar constitution. The gaseous atom is an ovoid body, within which a spirally-coiled snake-like body revolves at a high velocity, five brilliant points of light shining on the coils. The appearance given in the former diagram will be obtained by placing the five septets on one side on the top of those on the other, so that the ten become in appearance five, and thus doubling the whole, the doubling point leaving eleven duads on each side. The composition is, however, much better seen by flattening out the whole. On the proto level the two snakes separate and are clearly seen.

OXYGEN : Positive snake,	{ 55 spheres of 2 atoms + 5 disks of 7 atoms } ...	145
Negative snake	" ...	145
	Total ...	290
Atomic weight	...	15·87
Number weight $\frac{290}{18}$	...	16·11

CHROMIUM (Plate VIII., 5) " reverts to the ancestral type, " the tetrahedron ; the funnel is widened by the arrangement of its contents, three spheres forming its first ring, as compared with the units in beryllium and calcium, and the pairs in strontium and molybdenum. Two of these spheres are identical in their contents—two quintets (7 *f*), a quintet (7 *j*), and two quintets (7 *e*), *e* and *f* being to each other as object and image. The remaining sphere (7 *b*) is identical with the highest in the calcium funnel. The remaining two spheres, one below the other, are identical with the corresponding two spheres in calcium. The central globe, as regards its external segments, is again identical with that of calcium, but in the internal segments a six-atomed triangle (7 *k*) is substituted for the calcium four-atomed one (7 *e*).

CHROMIUM : 4 funnels of 210 atoms	...	840
Central globe	...	96
	Total ...	936
Atomic weight	...	51·74
Number weight $\frac{936}{18}$	...	52·00

MOLYBDENUM (Plate VIII., 6) very closely resembles strontium, differing from it only in the composition of the highest pair of spheres in the funnels and in the presence of a little sphere, containing two atoms only, in the middle of the central globe. The topmost spheres contain no less than eight subsidiary spheres within each ; the highest of these (7 *e*) has four atoms in it ; the next three have four, seven and four (7 *e g e*), respectively ; the next three are all septets, (7 *g*), and the last has four—making in all, for these two spheres 88 atoms, as against the 48 in corresponding spheres of strontium, making a difference of 160 in the four funnels.

MOLYBDENUM :	4 funnels of 408 atoms	...	1632
	Central globe	...	98
	Total	...	1730
	Atomic weight	...	95·26
	Number weight $\frac{1730}{18}$	...	96·11

II *a*. This group contains magnesium, zinc, cadmium, and mercury, with an empty disk between cadmium and mercury ; we did not examine mercury. All are diatomic, diamagnetic and positive ; the corresponding group consists of sulphur, selenium and tellurium, also all diatomic and diamagnetic, but negative. The same characteristics, of four funnels opening on the faces of a tetrahedron are found in all, but magnesium and sulphur have no central globe, and in cadmium and tellurium the globe has become a cross.

MAGNESIUM (Plate IX., 1) introduces us to a new arrangement : each group of three ovoids forms a ring, and the three rings are within a funnel ; at first glance, there are three bodies in the funnel ; on examination each of these is seen to consist of three, with other bodies, spheres, again within them. Apart from this, the composition is simple enough, all the ovoids being alike, and composed of a triplet, a septet and a duad.

MAGNESIUM :	4 funnels of 108 atoms	...	432
	Atomic weight	...	24·18
	Number weight $\frac{432}{18}$	...	24·00

ZINC (Plate IX., 2) also brings a new device : the funnel is of the same type as that of magnesium, while septets are substituted for the triplets, and 36 additional atoms are thus slipped in. Then we see four spikes, alternating with the funnels and pointing to the angles, each adding 144 atoms to the total. The spikes show the ten-atomed triangle, already met with in other metals, three very regular pillars, each with six spheres, containing two, three, four, four, three, two atoms, respectively. The supporting spheres are on

PLATE IX.

1

2

3

the model of the central globe, but contain more atoms. Funnels and spikes alike radiate from a simple central globe, in which five contained spheres are arranged crosswise, preparing for the fully developed cross of cadmium. The ends of the cross touch the bottoms of the funnels.

ZINC :	4 funnels of 144 atoms	...	576
	4 spikes of 144 atoms	...	576
	Central globe	...	18
		Total ...	1170
	Atomic weight	...	64·91
	Number weight $\frac{1170}{18}$	...	65·00

CADMIUM (Plate IX. 3) has an increased complexity of funnels ; the diagram shows one of the three similar segments which lie within the funnels as cylinders ; each of these contains four spheres, three pillars and three ovoids, like the spike of zinc turned upside down, and the zinc ten-atomed triangle changed into three ten-atomed ovoids. The centre-piece is a new form, though prefigured in the central globe of zinc.

CADMIUM :	{ 3 segments of 164 atoms = 492 { 4 funnels of 492 atoms }	...	1968
	Central body	...	48
		Total ...	2016
	Atomic weight	...	111·60
	Number weight $\frac{2016}{18}$	...	112·00

The corresponding negative group is headed by

SULPHUR (Plate X. 1), which, like magnesium, has no central globe, and consists simply of the zinc funnels, much less compressed than zinc but the same in composition.

SULPHUR :	4 funnels of 144 atoms	...	576
	Atomic weight	...	31·82
	Number weight $\frac{576}{18}$	...	32·00

SELENIUM (Plate X. 2) is distinguished by the exquisite peculiarity, already noticed, of a quivering star, floating across the mouth of each funnel, and dancing violently when a ray of light falls upon it. It is known that the conductivity of selenium varies with the intensity of the light falling upon it, and it may be that the star is in some way connected with its conductivity. It will be seen that the star is a very complicated body, and in each of its six points the two five-atomed spheres revolve round the seven-atomed cone. The bodies in the funnels resemble those in magnesium, but a reversed image of the top one is interposed between itself and the small duad, and each pair has its own enclosure. The central globe is the same as that of zinc.

PLATE X.

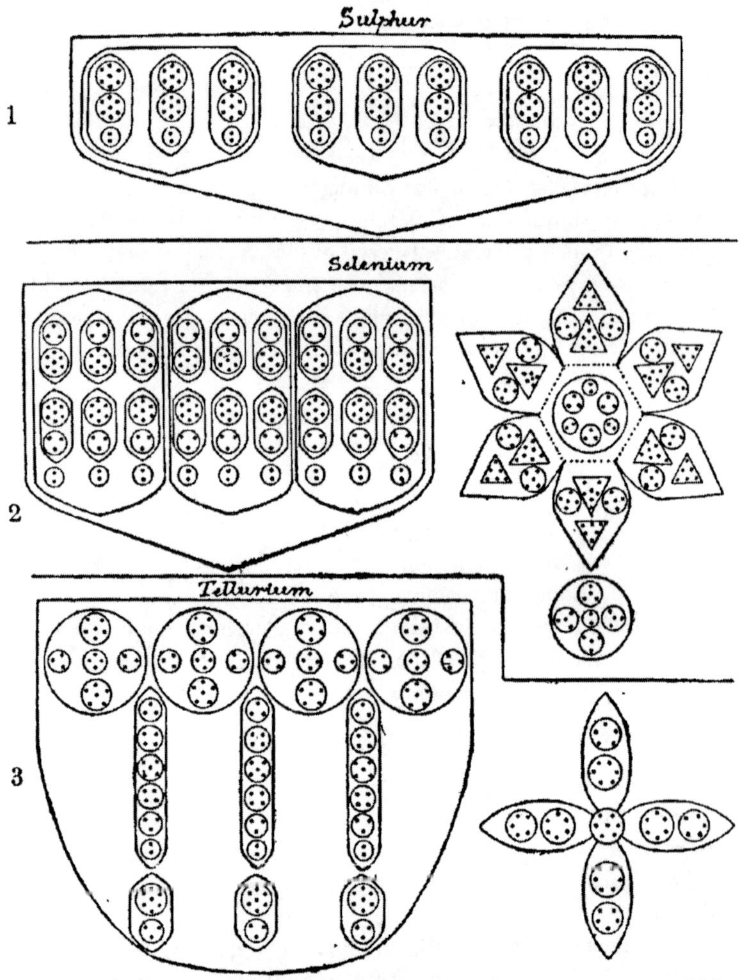

SELENIUM :	4 funnels of 198 atoms	...	792
	4 stars of 153 atoms	...	612
	Central globe	...	18
	Total	...	1422
	Atomic weight	...	78·58
	Number weight $\frac{1422}{18}$	...	79·00

TELLURIUM (Plate X. 3), it will be seen, closely resembles cadmium, and has three cylindrical segments—of which one is figured—making up the funnel. The contained bodies in the pillars run three, four, five, four, three, two, instead of starting with two; and a quartet replaces a duad in the globes above. The central cross only differs from that of cadmium in having a seven-atomed instead of a four-atomed centre. So close a similarity is striking.

TELLURIUM :	3 segments of 181 atoms = 543 4 funnels of 543 atoms	...	2172
	Central body	...	51
	Total	...	2223
	Atomic weight	...	126·64
	Number weight $\frac{2223}{18}$	...	123·50

VI.

We must now consider the ways in which the members of the tetrahedral groups break up, and as we proceed with this study, we shall find how continual are the repetitions, and how Nature, with a limited number of fundamental methods, creates by varied combinations her infinite variety of forms.

BERYLLIUM (PLATE III., 2, and VIII., 1).

Beryllium offers us four similar funnels and a central globe, and the proto-elements consist of these five bodies, set free. The funnel, released from pressure, assumes a spherical form, with its four ovoids spinning within it, and the central globe remains a sphere, containing a whirling cross. On the meta level, the ovoids are set free, and two from each funnel are seen to be positive, two negative—sixteen bodies in all, *plus* the cross, in which the resultant force-lines are changed, preparatory to its breaking into two duads on the hyper level. On that level, the decads disintegrate into two triplets and a quartet, the positive with the depressions inward, the negative with the depressions outward.

CALCIUM (PLATE VIII., 2).

The funnels, as usual, assume a spherical form on the proto level, and show, in each case, three spheres containing ovoids. These spheres, still on the proto level, break free from their containing funnel, as in the case of gold (p. 34), twelve bodies being thus iberated, while the central globe breaks up into eight segments, each of which becomes globular, and contains within it a 'cigar' and a somewhat heart-shaped body. Four spheres, each containing seven ten-atomed ovoids, are identical with those in beryllium, and can be followed in its diagram. Eight spheres, each containing five nine-atomed ovoids of a different type, set free, on the meta level, eighty duads—forty positive and forty negative—and forty quintets, which are identical with those in chlorine. On the hyper level, the duads become single atoms within a sphere, and the central atom from the quintet is also set free, one hundred and twenty in all. The remaining four atoms of the quintet divide into two duads.

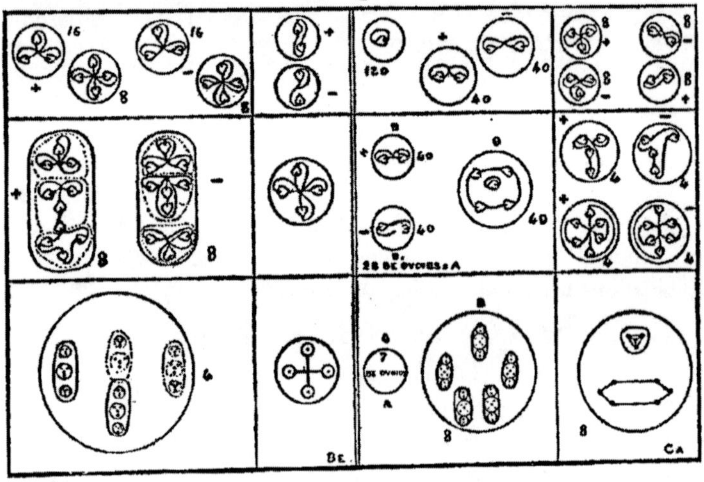

The central globe, dividing into eight, becomes eight six-atomed spheres on the meta, the 'cigar' behaving as usual, four 'cigars' being positive and four negative, and becoming dissociated into triplets; the four atoms within the heart shaped body appear as a tetrahedron, remain together on the meta level, and break up into duads on the hyper.

Strontium (Plate VIII., 3).

The third member of this group repeats the *a* groups of beryllium and the *b* groups of calcium, and they dissociate into the bodies already described under these respectively. The two upper globes in each funnel repeat each other, but each globe contains four smaller spheres showing three varieties of forms. The two marked *g*, which are repeated in the central globe as *h*, are seven-atomed, and appear as spheres or ovoids according to pressure. They are figured on p. 32, under iodine ; *e* and *f* are related as object and image, and we have already seen them in copper (pp. 21 and 32) ; in each case, as in copper, they unite into a ten-atomed figure ; on the meta level the pair of fours form a ring, and the remaining two atoms form a duad ; *i*, which repeats *f*, makes a ring with the fifth in the centre, as in the five-atomed *b* of calcium, as shown above. There is, thus, nothing new in strontium, but only repetitions of forms already studied.

OXYGEN (PLATE VIII., 4).

The disintegration of oxygen as given in 1895 may be repeated here, and the better presentation given on p. 36 renders it easier to follow the process. On the proto level the two 'snakes' divide ; the brilliant disks are seven-atomed, but are differently arranged, the positive snake having the atoms arranged as in the iodine ovoids, whereas the negative snake has them arranged as in a capital H. The snakes show the same extraordinary activity on the proto level as on the gaseous, twisting and writhing, darting and coiling. The

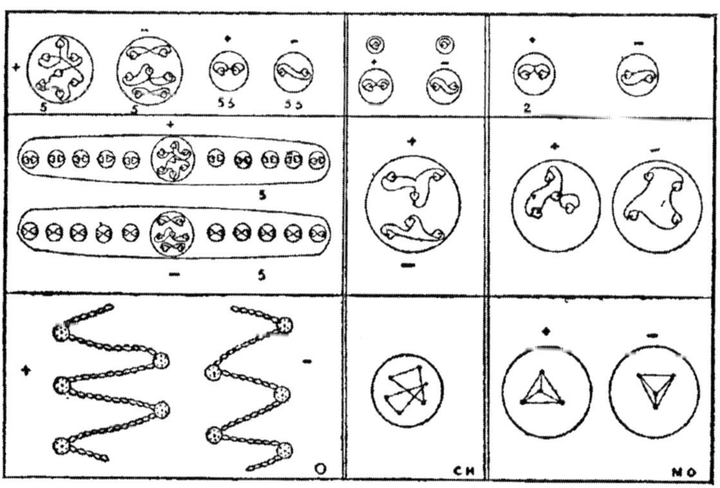

body of the snake is of two-atomed beads, positive and negative. On the meta level the snakes break into ten fragments, each consisting of a disk, with six beads on one side and five on the other, remaining as lively as the original snake. They shiver into their constituent disks, and beads on the hyper level, there yielding the ten disks, five positive and five negative, and the 110 beads, fifty-five positive and fifty-five negative.

Chromium (Plate VIII., 5).

When we go on to chromium and molybedenum, we return to our familiar funnels and central globes, and the secondary spheres within the funnels—quickly set free, as before, on the proto level—give us no new combinations in their contained spheres and ovoids. The *a* of beryllium, the *b* of calcium and strontium, and *d* of calcium, the *e* and *f* of strontium, are all there ; *j* in chromium is the same as the central sphere in the *b* ovoid. In the central globe, *k* is a pair of triangles as in hydrogen, consisting of only six atoms, which on the meta level revolve round each other, and break up into two duads and two units on the hyper.

Molybedenum (Plate VIII., 6).

Molybdenum presents us with only two new forms, and these are merely four-atomed tetrahedra, occurring in pairs, as object and image. All the other bodies have already been analysed.

II *a*. We come now to the second great tetrahedral group, which though very much complicated, is yet, for the most part, a repetition of familiar forms.

Magnesium (Plate IX., 1).

We are still among tetrahedra, so have to do with four funnels, but each funnel contains three rings, and each ring three ovoids ; on the proto level a triple dissociation takes place, for the funnels let free the rings as large spheres, in each of which rotate three twelve-atomed ovoids, and then the ovoids break loose from the spheres, and themselves become spherical, so that we have finally thirty-six proto compounds from the tetrahedron. On the meta level the contained bodies, a triplet, Mg *a*, a septet, Mg *b*, and a duad, Mg *c*, are set free from each globe, thus yielding one hundred and eight meta compounds. On the hyper level the triplet becomes a duad and a unit ; the duad becomes two units ; and the septet a triplet and a quartet.

ZINC (PLATE IX., 2).

We can leave aside the funnel, for the only difference between it and the magnesium funnel is the substitution of a second septet for the triplet, and the septet is already shown in the magnesium diagram. We have, therefore, only to consider the spikes, pointing to the angles of the enclosing tetrahedron, and the central globe. These are set free on the proto level and the spikes immediately release their contents, yielding thus thirty-two separate bodies.

The triangular arrangement at the top of the spike is the same as occurs in copper (*b* on p. 32), and can be there followed. One of the three similar pillars is shown in the accompanying diagram under Zn *a*. The compressed long oval becomes a globe, with six bodies revolving within it in a rather peculiar way : the quartets turn round each other in the middle ; the triplets revolve round them in a slanting ellipse ; the duads do the same on an ellipse slanting at an angle with the first, somewhat as in gold (*a* and *b*, p. 24). The spheres within the globes at the base of the spikes, Zn *b*, behave as a cross—the cross is a favorite device in the II *a* groups. Finally, the central globe, Zn *e*, follows the same cruciform line of disintegration.

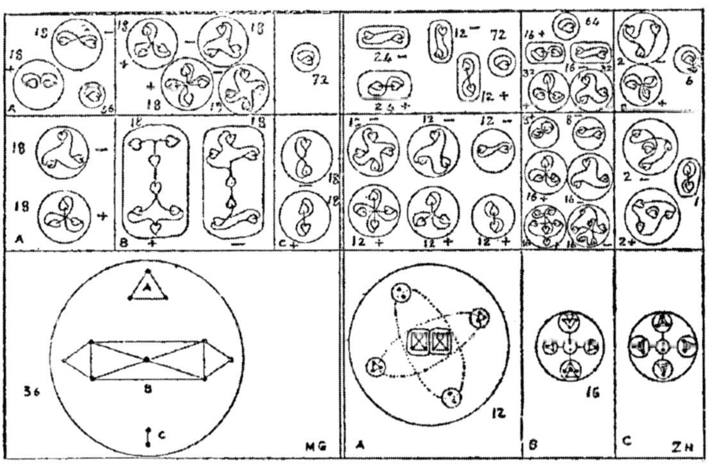

Cadmium (Plate IX., 3).

Cadmium follows very closely on the lines of zinc ; the pillars of the zinc spike are reproduced in the rings of the cadmium funnel ; the globes are also the globes of cadmium ; so neither of these needs attention. We have only to consider the three ten-atomed ovoids, which are substituted for the one ten-atomed triangle of zinc, and the central cross. The ovoids become spheres, (Cd *a*, *b*,) the contained

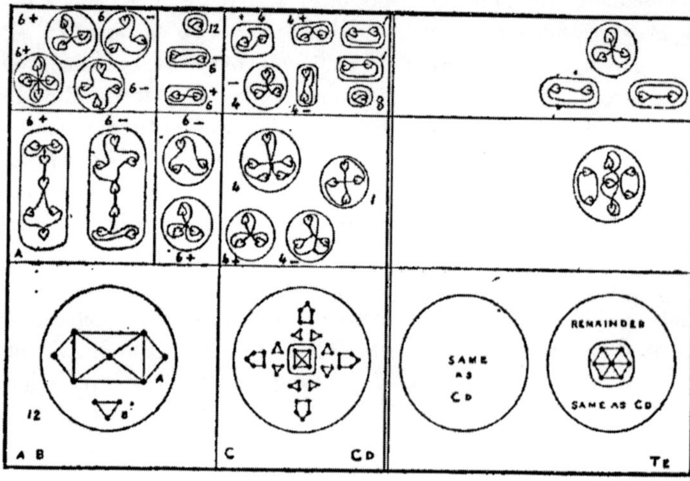

bodies revolving within them, *a* whirling on a diameter of the sphere, cutting it in halves, as it were, and *b* whirling round it at right angles ; the cross also becomes a sphere, (Cd *c*), but the cruciform type is maintained within it by the relative positions of the contained spheres in their revolution. The subsequent stages are shown in the diagram.

Sulphur (Plate X., 1).

Sulphur has nothing new, but shows only the funnels already figured in magnesium, with the substitution of a second septet for the triplet, as in zinc.

Selenium (Plate X., 2).

The funnel of selenium is a re-arrangement of the twelve-atomed ovoids of magnesium and the ten-atomed ovoids of cadmium. The funnels, on disintegrating, set free twelve groups, each containing nine spheres. On the meta level, the ten-atomed bodies are set free, and the twelve-atomed divide into duads and decads, thus yielding seventy-two decads and thirty-six duads ; the duads, however, at once recombine into hexads, thus giving only twelve meta elements, or eighty-four in all from the funnels. The central globe holds together on the proto level, but yields five meta elements. The star also at first remains a unit on the proto level, and then shoots off into seven bodies, the centre keeping together, and the six points becoming spheres, within which the two cones, base to base, whirl in the centre, and the globes circle round them. On the meta level all the thirty bodies contained in the star separate from each other, and go on their independent ways.

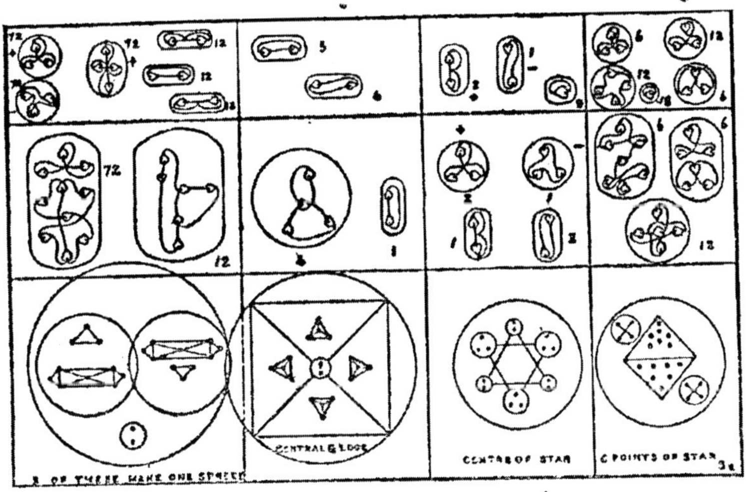

Selenium offers a beautiful example of the combination of simple elements into a most exquisite whole.

TELLURIUM (PLATE X., 3).

Tellurium very closely resembles cadmium, and they are, therefore placed on the same diagram. The pillars are the same as in chlorine and its congeners, with a duad added at the base. The ten-atomed ovoid is the same as in cadmium and follows the same course in breaking up. It would be interesting to know why this duad remains as a duad in selenium and breaks up into a septad and triad in the other members of the group. It may be due to the greater pressure to which it is subjected in selenium, or there may be some other reason. The cross in tellurium is identical with that in cadmium, except that the centre is seven-atomed instead of four-atomed.

VII.

III AND III*a*. THE CUBE GROUPS.

We have here four groups to consider, all the members of which are triads, and have six funnels, opening on the six faces of a cube.

III. Boron, scandium and yttrium were examined ; they are all triatomic, paramagnetic, and positive. The corresponding group consists of nitrogen, vanadium and niobium ; they are triatomic, paramagnetic, and negative. We have not examined the remaining members of these groups. In these two groups nitrogen dominates, and in order to make the comparison easy the nitrogen elements are figured on both Plate XI and Plate XII. It will be seen that scandium and yttrium, of the positive group, differ only in details from vanadium and niobium, of the negative group ; the ground-plan on which they are built is the same. We noted a similar close resemblance between the positive strontium and the negative molybdenum.

BORON (Plate III, 4, and Plate XI, 1). We have here the simplest form of the cube ; the funnels contain only five bodies—four six-atomed ovoids and one six-atomed 'cigar.' The central globe has but four five-atomed spheres. It is as simple in relation to its congeners as is beryllium to its group-members.

BORON :	6 funnels of 30 atoms	180
	Central Globe	20
	Total ...	200

Atomic Weight	... 10·86
Number Weight $\frac{200}{18}$	... 11·11

SCANDIUM (Plate XI, 2). For the first time we meet funnels of different types, A and B., three of each kind ; A appear to be positive and B negative, but this must be stated with reserve.

In A the boron funnel is reproduced, the ' cigar ' having risen above its companion ovoids ; but the most important matter to note in respect to this funnel is our introduction to the body marked *a* 110. This body was observed by us first in nitrogen, in 1895, and

PLATE XI.

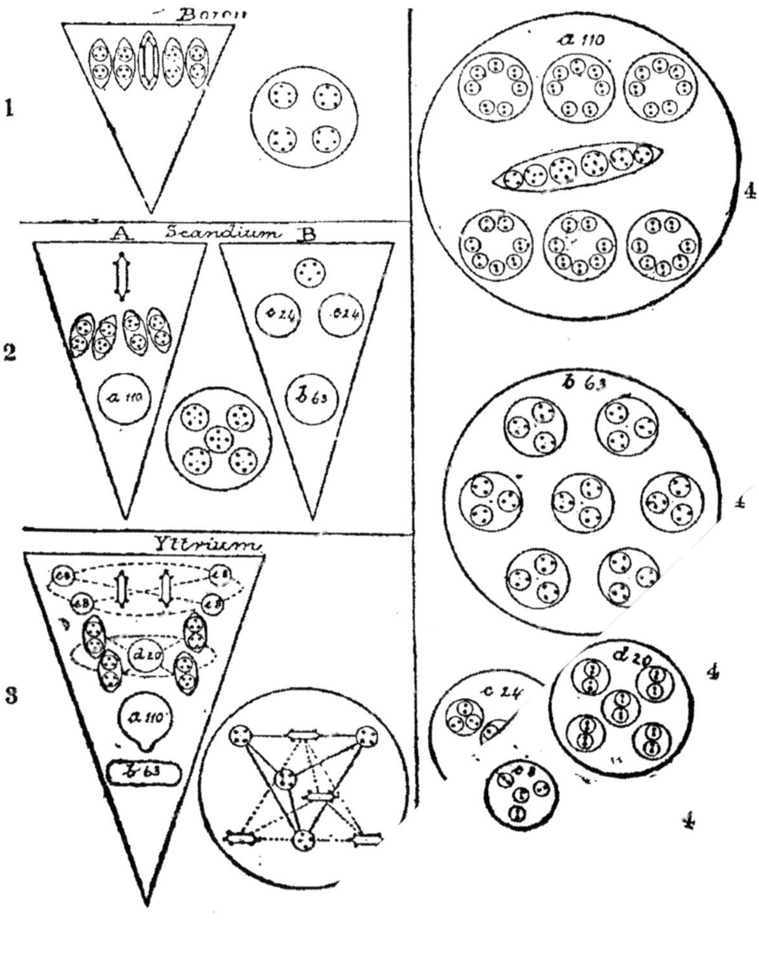

we gave it the name of the 'nitrogen balloon,' for in nitrogen it takes the balloon form, which it also often assumes in other gaseous elements. Here it appears as a sphere—the form always assumed on the proto level—and it will be seen, on reference to the detailed diagram 4 *a*, to be a complicated body, consisting of six fourteen-atomed globes arranged round a long ovoid containing spheres with three, four, six, six, four, three, atoms respectively. It will be observed that this balloon appears in every member of these two groups, except boron.

The B funnel runs largely to triads, *c* and *b*, *b* (see 4 *b*) having not only a triadic arrangement of spheres within its contained globes, but each sphere has also a triplet of atoms. In *c* (see 4 *c*) there is a triadic arrangement of spheres, but each contains duads. B is completed by a five-atomed sphere at the top of the funnel. It should be noted that *a*, *b* and *c* all are constituents of nitrogen.

The central globe repeats that of boron, with an additional four-atomed sphere in the middle.

SCANDIUM :	3 funnels (A) of 140 atoms	...	420
	3 „ (B) of 116 „	...	348
	Central Globe	...	24
	Total	...	792
	Atomic Weight	...	43·78
	Number Weight $\frac{792}{18}$	...	44·00

YTTRIUM (Plate XI, 3). Here we have a quite new arrangement of bodies within the funnel—the funnel being of one type only. Two 'cigars' whirl on their own axes in the centre near the top, while round th[e] eight-atomed globes (see 4 *e*) chase each other in a circle seems co[n]...spinning madly on their own axes—this axial spinning in the funnel all contained bodies—all the time. Lower down a nitrogen ... [s]imilar arrangement is seen, with a globe (see 4 *d*)— replacing the gl... placing the 'cigars,' and six-atomed ovoids

The 'nitrogen ... now showing its ... ' occupies the third place in the funnel, (see 4 *b*) of scandium ... e in combination, while the *b* globe ... lengthened form below it.

The central globe ... with two tetrahedra, recalling one of the combinations in ... te VII *d*, p. 24), and differing from that only by the substitution of two quartets for the two triplets in gold.

One funnel of yttrium contains exactly the same number of atoms as is contained in a gaseous atom of nitrogen. Further, *a*, *b*, and *d* are all nitrogen elements. We put on record these facts, without trying to draw any conclusions from them. Some day, we —or others—may find out their significance, and trace through them obscure relations.

YTTRIUM :	6 funnels of 261 atoms	...	1566
	Central Globe	...	40
	Total	...	1606
	Atomic Weight	...	88·34
	Number Weight $\frac{1606}{18}$	...	89·22

The corresponding negative group, of nitrogen, vanadium and niobium, is rendered particularly interesting by the fact, that it is headed by nitrogen, which—like the air, of which it forms so large a part—pervades so many of the bodies we are studying. What is there in nitrogen which renders it so inert as to conveniently dilute the fiery oxygen and make it breathable, while it is so extraordinarily active in some of its compounds that it enters into the most powerful explosives? Some chemist of the future, perhaps, will find the secret in the arrangement of its constituent parts, which we are able only to describe.

NITROGEN (Plate XII, 1) does not assume the cubical form of its relatives, but is in shape like an egg. Referring again to our 1895 investigations, I quote from them. The balloon-shaped body (see 4 *a*) floats in the middle of the egg, containing six small spheres in two horizontal rows, and a long ovoid in the midst; this balloon-shaped body is positive, and is drawn down towards the negative body *b* (see 4 *b*) with its seven-contained spheres, each of which has nine atoms within it—three triads. Four spheres are seen, in addition to the two larger bodies; two of these (see 4 *d*), each containing five smaller globes, are positive, and two (see 4 *c*) containing four smaller globes, are negative.

NITROGEN :	Balloon	...	110
	Oval	...	63
	2 bodies of 20 atoms	...	40
	2 „ „ 24 „	...	48
	Total	...	261

Atomic Weight ... 14·01
Number Weight $\frac{261}{18}$ ... 14·50

VANADIUM (Plate XII, 2) closely follows scandium, having two types of funnels. Funnel A only differs from that of scandium by having a globe (see 4 *d*) inserted in the ring of four ovoids; funnel B has a six-atomed, instead of a five-atomed globe at the top, and slips a third globe containing twenty atoms (see 4 *d*) between the

PLATE XII.

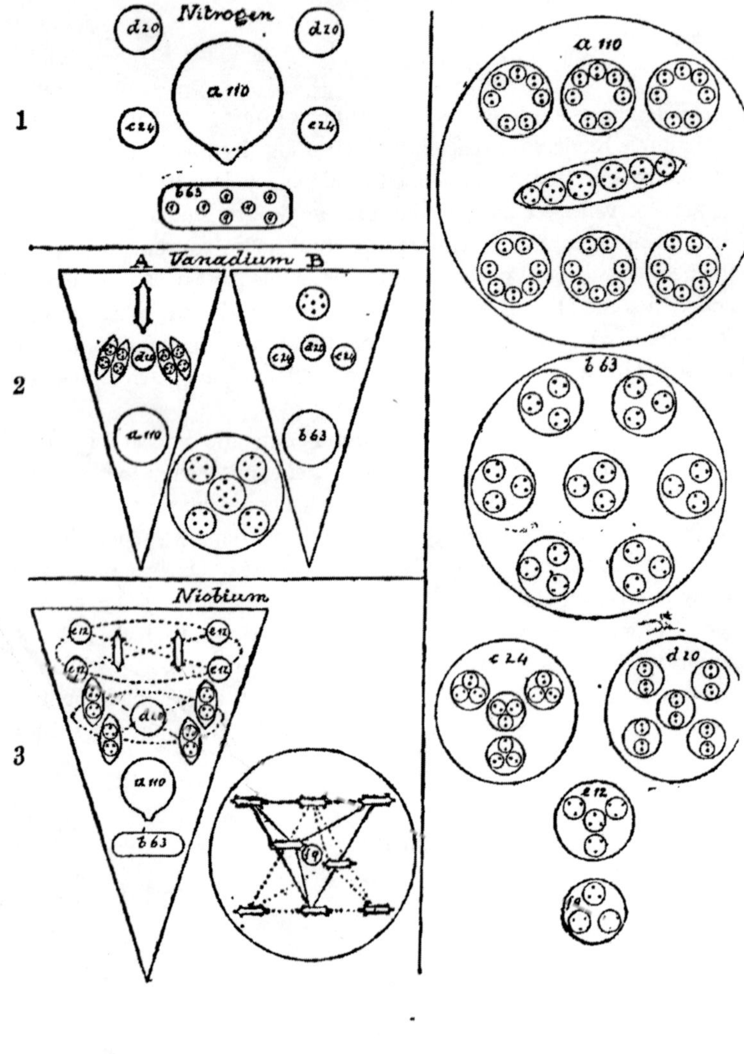

two identical with those of scandium (see 4 *c*). The central globe has seven atoms in its middle body instead of four. In this way does vanadium succeed in overtopping scandium by 126 atoms.

VANADIUM :	3 funnels (A) of 160 atoms	...	480
	3 ,, (B) ,, 137 ,,	...	411
	Central Globe	...	27
	Total	...	918
	Atomic Weight	...	50·84
	Number Weight $\frac{918}{18}$	...	51·00

NIOBIUM (Plate XII, 3) is as closely related to yttrium as is vanadium to scandium. The little globes that scamper round the 'cigars' contain twelve atoms instead of eight (see 4 *e*).

The rest of the funnel is the same. In the central globe both the tetrahedra have 'cigars,' and a central nine-atomed globe spins round in the centre (see 4 *f*), seventeen atoms being thus added.

NIOBIUM :	6 funnels of 277 atoms	...	1662
	Central Globe	...	57
	Total	...	1719
	Atomic Weight	...	93·25
	Number Weight $\frac{1719}{18}$	...	95·50

III *a*. Aluminium, gallium and indium were examined from this group. They are triatomic, diamagnetic, and positive. The corresponding group contains phosphorus, arsenic and antimony : bismuth also belongs to it, but was not examined ; they are triatomic, diamagnetic and negative. They have no central globes.

ALUMINIUM (Plate XIII, 1), the head of the group, is, as usual, simple. There are six similar funnels, each containing eight ovoids, below which is a globe.

ALUMINIUM :	6 funnels of 81 atoms	...	486
	Atomic Weight	...	26·91
	Number Weight $\frac{486}{18}$	...	27·00

GALLIUM (Plate XIII, 2) has two segments in every funnel ; in the segment to the left a 'cigar' balances a globe, equally six-atomed, in that of the right, and the globes to right and left are four-atomed as against three-atomed. In the next row, the smaller contained globes have six atoms as against four, and the cones have respectively seven and five. By these little additions the left hand funnel boasts one hundred and twelve atoms as against ninety-eight.

GALLIUM :	Left segment 112 atoms Right segment 98 ,,	} = 210	
	6 funnels of 210 atoms	...	1260
	Atomic Weight	...	69·50
	Number Weight $\frac{1260}{18}$	...	70·00

PLATE XIII.

INDIUM (Plate XIII, 3) repeats the segments of gallium exactly, save in the substitution of a sixteen-atomed body for the seven-atomed cone of the left hand segment, and a fourteen-atomed body for the five-atomed corresponding one in gallium. But each funnel now has three segments instead of two ; three funnels out of the six contain two segments of type A and one of type B ; the remaining three contain two of type B, and one of type A.

INDIUM :		
	Segment A 121 atoms	
	Segment B 107 ,,	
	3 funnels of 2 A and 1 B ([242 + 107] 3) ...	1047
	3 ,, ,, 2 B and 1 A ([214 + 121] 3) ...	1005
	Total ...	2052
	Atomic Weight	... 114·05
	Number Weight $\frac{2052}{18}$	... 114·00

The corresponding negative group, phosphorus, arsenic, and antimony, run on very similar lines to those we have just examined.

PHOSPHORUS (Plate XIV, 1) offers us a very curious arrangement of atoms, which will give some new forms in breaking up. Two segments are in each funnel, in fact the only two of group III *a* which do not show this arrangement, or a modification thereof, are aluminium and arsenic.

PHOSPHORUS :		
	Left segment 50 atoms, Right segment 43 ,, } = 93	
	6 funnels of 93 atoms	... 558
	Atomic Weight	... 30·77
	Number Weight $\frac{558}{18}$	... 31·00

ARSENIC (Plate XIV, 2) resembles aluminium in having eight internal sub-divisions in a funnel, and the ovoids which form the top ring are identical, save for a minute difference that in aluminium the ovoids stand the reverse way from those in arsenic. It will be noted that in the former the top and bottom triangles of atoms have the apices upwards, and the middle one has its apex downwards. In arsenic, the top and bottom ones point downwards, and the middle one upwards. Arsenic inserts sixteen spheres between the ovoids and globe shown in aluminium, and thus adds no less than one hundred and forty-four atoms to each funnel.

ARSENIC :		
	6 funnels of 225 atoms	... 1350
	Atomic Weight	... 74·45
	Number Weight $\frac{1350}{18}$	... 75·00

PLATE XIV.

1

2

3

ANTIMONY (Plate XIV, 3) is a close copy of indium, and the arrangement of types A and B in the funnels is identical. In the middle rings of both A and B, a triplet is substituted for a unit at the centre of the larger globe. In the lowest body of type A the 'cigar' has vanished, and is represented by a seven-atomed crystalline form.

ANTIMONY : Segment A 128 atoms
Segment B 113 atoms

3 funnels of 2 A and 1 B ([256 + 113]3) ...	1107
3 „ „ 2 B and 1 A ([226 + 128]3) ...	1056
Total ...	2163
Atomic Weight ...	119·34
Number Weight ..	120·16

VIII.

BORON (PLATE III., 4 and PLATE XI., 1).

The disintegration of boron is very simple : the funnels are set free and assume the spherical form, showing a central 'cigar' and four globes each containing two triplets. The central globe is also set free with its four quintets, and breaks at once in two. On the meta level the 'cigar' breaks up as usual, and the triplets separate. On the hyper level, the 'cigar' follows its usual course, and the triplets become duads and units. The globe forms two quintets on the meta level, and these are resolved into triplets and duads.

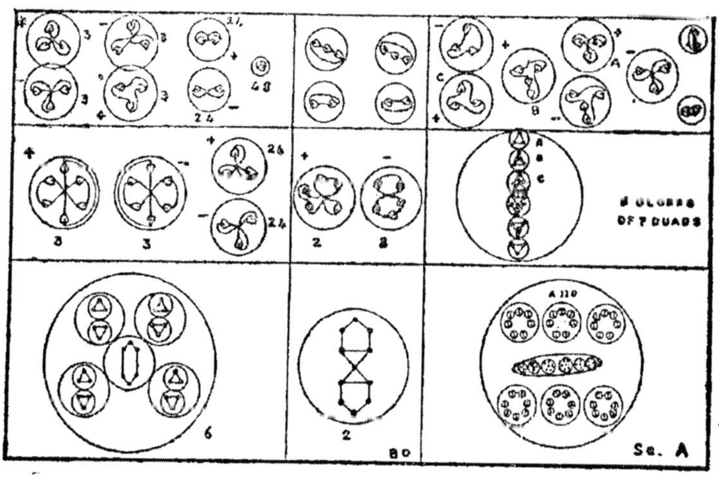

SCANDIUM (PLATE XI., 2).

In funnel A the 'cigar' and the ovoids behave as in boron, but the 'balloon,' *a* 110 (XI., 4) escapes from the funnel as it changes to a sphere, and holds together on the proto level ; on the meta, it yields six globes each containing seven duads, and these are all set free as duads on the hyper level ; the ovoid is also set free on the meta level becoming a sphere, and on the hyper level liberates its contained bodies, as two triplets, two quartets and two sextets.

In funnel B there is a quintet, that behaves like those in the globe of boron, on escaping from the funnel, in which the bodies remain on the proto level, with the exception of *b* 63, which escapes. On the meta level, *c* (Plate XI., 4) *c* assumes a tetrahedral form with six atoms at each point, and these hold together as sextets on the hyper level. At the meta stage, *b* (Plate XI, 4 *b*) sets free seven nine-atomed bodies, which become free triplets on the hyper. The central globe shows a cross at its centre, with the four quintets whirling round it, on the proto level. On the meta, the quintets are set free, and follow the boron type, while the cross becomes a quartet on the meta level, and two duads on the hyper.

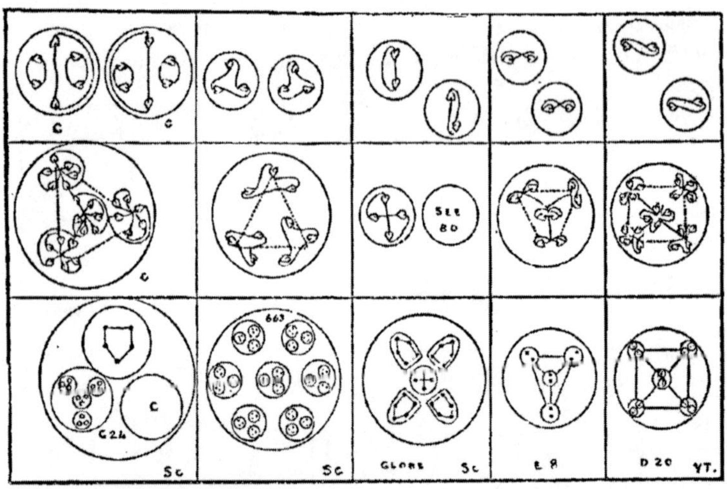

YTTRIUM (PLATE XI., 3).

In yttrium, on the proto level, *a* 110 and *b* 63 both escape from the funnel, and behave as in scandium. The ovoids and 'cigars,' set free on the meta level, behave as in boron. The central globe breaks up as in gold (pp. 34 and 35), four quartets being set free insead of two quartets and two triplets. We have only to consider *e* 8 and *d* 20 (Plate XI., 4). *E* 8 is a tetrahedral arrangement of duads on the meta level, set free as duads on the hyper. *D* 20 is an arrangement of pairs of duads at the angles of a square-based pyramid on the meta, and again free duads on the hyper.

NITROGEN (PLATE XII., 1).

Nitrogen has nothing new to show us, all its constituents having appeared in scandium and yttrium.

VANADIUM (PLATE XII., 2).

The A funnel of vanadium repeats the A funnel of scandium, with the addition of *d* 20, already studied. In the B funnel scandium B is repeated, with an addition of *d* 20 and a sextet for a quintet; the sextet is the *c* of the 'nitrogen balloon.' The central globe follows boron, save that it has a septet for its centre; this was figured in iodine (p. 32).

NIOBIUM (PLATE XII., 3).

Niobium only differs from yttrium by the introduction of triplets for duads in *e*; on the meta level we have therefore triplets, and on the hyper, each triplet yields a duad and a unit. The only other difference is in the central globe. The tetrahedra separate as usual, but liberate eight 'cigars' instead of four with four quartets; the central body is simple, becoming three triads at the angles of a triangle on the meta level, and three duads and three units on the hyper.

ALUMINIUM (PLATE XIII., 1).

The funnels let go the globes, but the eight ovoids remain within them, so that seven bodies are let loose on the proto level. When the ovoids are set free at the meta stage they become spherical and a nine-atomed body is produced, which breaks up into triangles on the hyper level. The globe becomes a cross at the meta stage, with one atom from the duads at each arm in addition to its own, and these form four duads on the hyper, and a unit from the centre.

GALLIUM (PLATE XIII., 2).

In gallium the funnel disappears on the proto level, setting free its two contained segments, each of which forms a cylinder, thus yielding twelve bodies on the proto level. On the meta, the three upper globes in each left hand segment are set free, and soon vanish, each liberating a cigar and two septets, the quartet and triad uniting. On the hyper the quartet yields two duads but the triangle persists. The second set of bodies divide on the meta level, forming a sextet and a cross with a duad at each arm; these on the hyper level divide into two triangles, four duads and a unit. The seven-atomed cone becomes two triangles united by a single atom, and on the meta level these form a ring round the unit; on the hyper they form three duads and a unit.

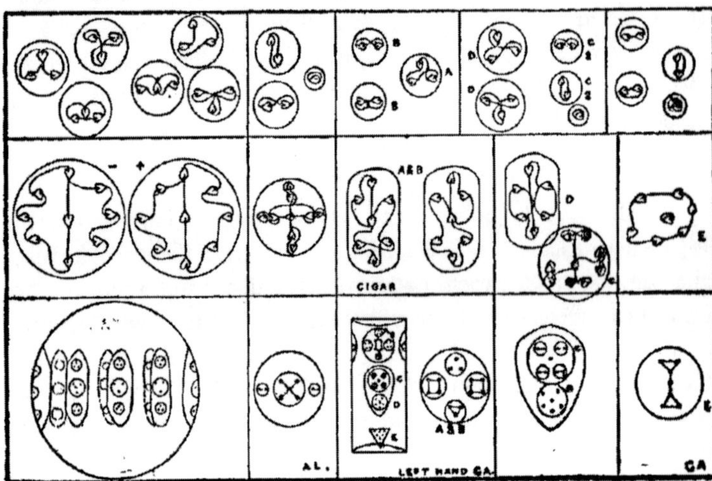

In the right hand segment, the same policy is followed, the four triads becoming two sextets, while the central body adds a third to the number. The second ring has a quartet instead of the sextet, but otherwise breaks up as does that of the left; the quintet at the base follows that of boron.

Indium (Plate XIII., 3).

The complication of three segments of different types in each funnel does not affect the process of breaking up, and indium needs little attention. A is exactly the same as the left hand funnel of gallium, save for the substitution of a globe containing the familiar 'cigar' and two square-based pyramids. B is the same as the right hand funnel of gallium, except that its lowest body consists of two square-based pyramids and a tetrahedron. All these are familiar.

PHOSPHORUS (PLATE XIV., 1).

The atoms in the six similar spheres in the segments of the phosphorus funnel are arranged on the eight angles of a cube, and the central one is attached to all of them. On the meta level five of the nine atoms hold together and place themselves on the angles of a square-based pyramid ; the remaining four set themselves on the angle of a tetrahedron. They yield, on the hyper level, two triads, a duad, and a unit. The remaining bodies are simple and familiar.

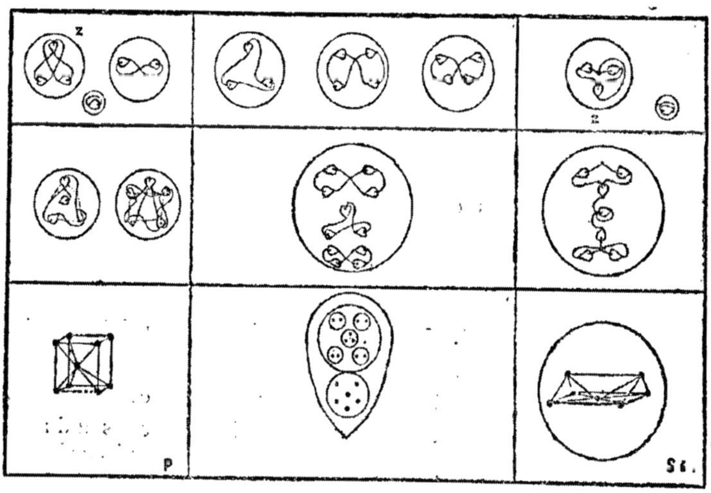

ARSENIC (PLATE XIV., 2).

Arsenic shows the same ovoids and globe as have already been broken up in aluminium (see *ante*) ; the remaining sixteen spheres form nine-atomed bodies on the meta level, all similar to those of aluminium, thus yielding twelve positive and twelve negative ; the globe also yields a nine-atomed body, twenty-five bodies of nine.

ANTIMONY (Plate XIV, 3).

Antimony follows closely in the track of gallium and indium, the upper ring of spheres being identical. In the second ring, a triplet is substituted for the unit, and this apparently throws the cross out of gear, and we have a new eleven-atomed figure, which breaks up into a triplet and two quartets on the hyper level. The lowest seven-atomed sphere of the three at the base, is the same as we met with in copper.

IX.

IV. The Octahedral Groups.

These groups are at the turns of the spiral in Sir William Crookes' lemniscates (see p. 12). On the one side is carbon, with below it titanium and zirconium; on the other silicon, with germanium and tin. The characteristic form is an octohedron, rounded at the angles and a little depressed between the faces in consequence of the rounding; in fact, we did not, at first, recognise it as an octohedron, and we called it the 'corded bale,' the nearest likeness that struck us. The members of the group are all tetrads, and have eight funnels, opening on the eight faces of the octohedron. The first group is paramagnetic and positive; the corresponding one is diamagnetic and negative. The two groups are not closely allied in composition, though both titanium and tin have in common the five intersecting tetrahedra at their respective centres.

Carbon (Plate III., 5 and XV., 1) gives us the fundamental octohedral form, which becomes so masked in titanium and zirconium. As before said (p. 14), the protrusion of the arms in these suggests the old Rosicrucian symbol of the cross and rose, but they show at their ends the eight carbon funnels with their characteristic contents, and thus justify their relationship. The funnels are in pairs, one of each pair showing three 'cigars,' and having as its fellow a funnel in which the middle 'cigar' is truncated, thus losing one atom. Each 'cigar' has a leaf-like body at its base, and in the centre of the octohedron is a globe containing four atoms, each within its own wall; these lie on the dividing lines of the faces, and each holds a pair of the funnels together. It seems as though this atom had been economically taken from the 'cigar' to form a link. This will be more clearly seen when we come to separate the parts from each other. It will be noticed that the atoms in the 'leaves' at the base vary in arrangement, being alternately in a line and in a triangle.

CARBON : One pair of funnels $\begin{cases} \text{left } 27 \\ \text{right } 26 = 54 \\ \text{centre } 1 \end{cases}$

4 pairs of funnels of 54 atoms	...	216
Atomic Weight	...	11·91
Number Weight $\frac{216}{18}$	...	12·00

PLATE XV.

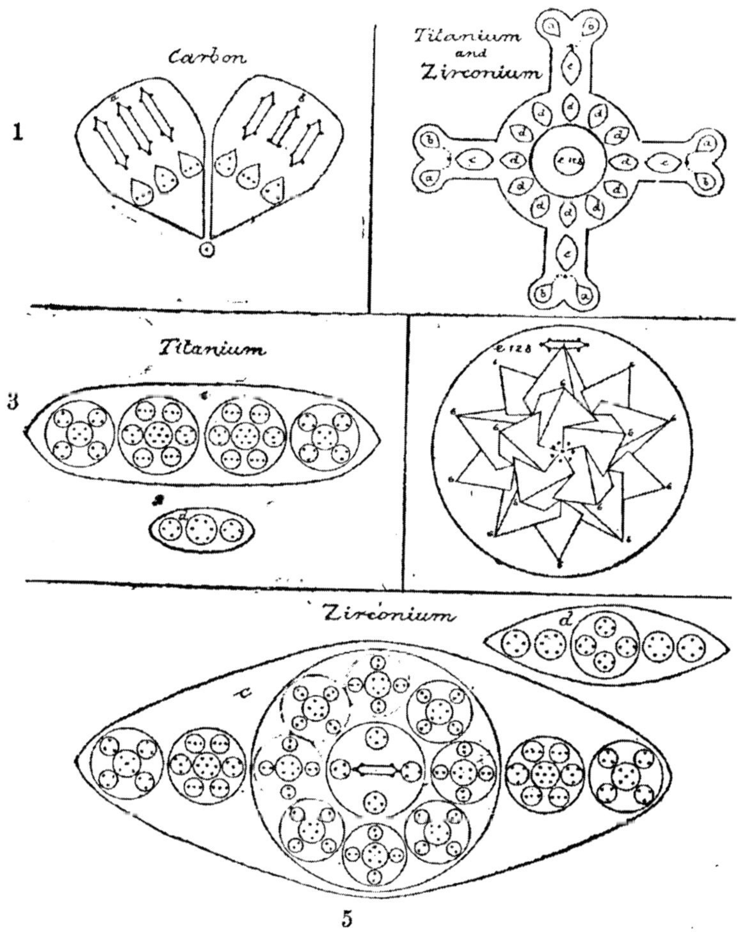

TITANIUM (Plate III., 6 and XV., 2) has a complete carbon atom distributed over the ends of its four arms, a pair of funnels with their linking atom, being seen in each. Then, in each arm, comes the elaborate body shown as 3*c*, with its eighty-eight atoms. A ring of twelve ovoids (3*d*) each holding within itself fourteen atoms, distributed among three contained globes—two quartets and a sextet—is a new device for crowding in material. Lastly comes the central body (4*e*) of five intersecting tetrahedra, with a 'cigar' at each of their twenty points—of which only fifteen can be shown in the diagram—and a ring of seven atoms round an eighth, that forms the minute centre of the whole. Into this elaborate body one hundred and twenty-eight atoms are built.

Titanium :	One Carbon Atom	...	216
	4 *c* of 88 Atoms	...	352
	12 *d* of 14 ,,	...	168
	Central Globe	...	128
	Total	...	864
	Atomic Weight	...	47·74
	Number Weight $\frac{864}{18}$	...	48·00

ZIRCONIUM (Plate XV., 3) has exactly the same outline as titanium, the carbon atom is similarly distributed, and the central body is identical. Only in 5 *c* and *d* do we find a difference on comparing them with 4 *c* and *d*. The *c* ovoid in zirconium shows no less than fifteen secondary globes within the five contained in the ovoid, and these, in turn, contain altogether sixty-nine smaller spheres, with two hundred and twelve atoms within them, arranged in pairs, triplets, quartets, quintets, a sextet and septets. Finally, the ovoids of the ring are also made more elaborate, showing thirty-six atoms instead of fourteen. In this way the clever builders have piled up in zirconium no less than 1624 atoms.

Zirconium:	One Carbon Atom	...	216
	4 *c* of 212 Atoms	...	848
	12 *d* of 36 ,,	...	432
	Central Globe	...	128
	Total	...	1624
	Atomic Weight	...	89.85
	Number Weight	...	90·22

SILICON (Plate XVI., 1) is at the head of the group which corresponds to carbon on the opposite turn of the lemniscate. It has the usual eight funnels, containing four ovoids in a circle, and a truncated 'cigar' but no central body of any kind. All the funnels are alike.

SILICON :	8 funnels of 65 atoms	...	520
	Atomic Weight	...	28·18
	Number Weight $\frac{520}{18}$	...	28·88

PLATE XVI.

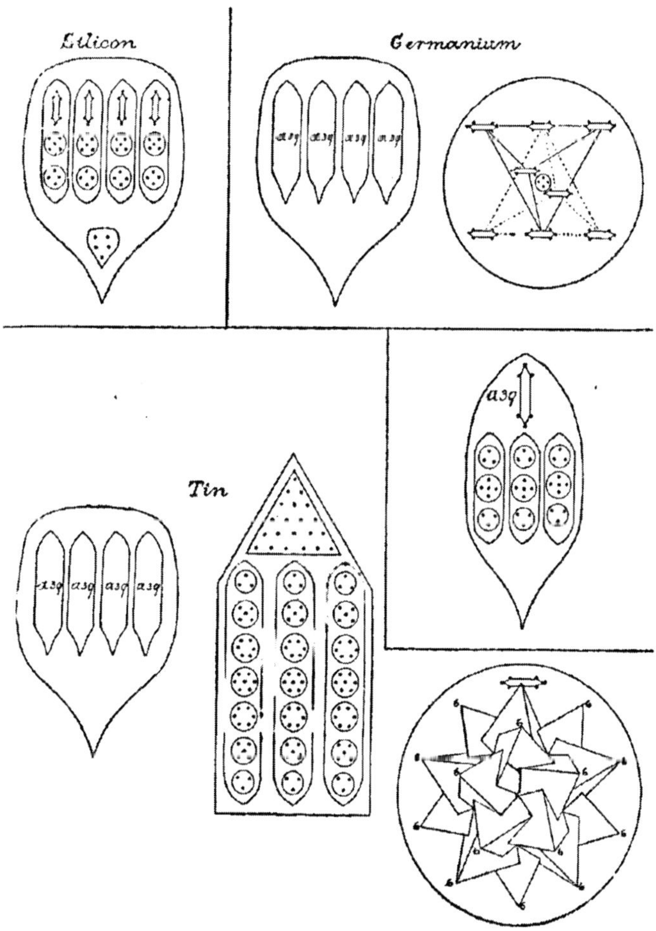

GERMANIUM (Plate XVI., 2) shews the eight funnels, containing each four segments (XVI., 4), within which are three ovoids and a 'cigar'. In this case the funnels radiate from a central globe, formed of two intersecting tetrahedra, with 'cigars' at each point enclosing a four-atomed globe.

GERMANIUM :	8 funnels of 156 atoms	...	1248
	Central Globe	...	52
		Total ...	1300
	Atomic Weight	...	71·93
	Number Weight $\frac{1300}{18}$	...	72·22

TIN (Plate XVI., 3) repeats the funnel of germanium, and the central globe we met with in titanium, of five intersecting tetrahedra, carrying twenty 'cigars'; the latter, however, omits the eight-atomed centre of the globe that was found in titanium, and hence has one hundred and twenty atoms therein instead of one hundred and twenty-eight. Tin, to make room for the necessary increase of atoms, adopts the system of spikes, which we met with in zinc (see p. 40 Plate IX., 2); these spikes, like the funnels, radiate from the central globe, but are only six in number. The twenty-one-atomed cone at the head of the spike we have already seen in silver, and we shall again find it in iridium and platinum; the pillars are new in detail though not in principle, the contained globes yielding a series of a triplet, quintet, sextet, septet, sextet, quintet, triplet.

TIN :	8 funnels of 156 atoms	...	1248
	6 spikes of 126 „	...	756
	Central Globe	...	120
		Total ...	2124
	Atomic Weight	...	118·10
	Number Weight $\frac{2124}{18}$	...	118·00

V. THE BARS GROUPS.

Here, for the first time, we find ourselves a little at issue with the accepted system of chemistry. Fluorine stands at the head of a group—called the inter-periodic—whereof the remaining members are (see Crookes' table, p. 12) manganese, iron, cobalt, nickel ; ruthenium, rhodium, palladium ; osmium, iridium, platinum. If we take all these as group V., we find that fluorine and

PLATE XVII.

2

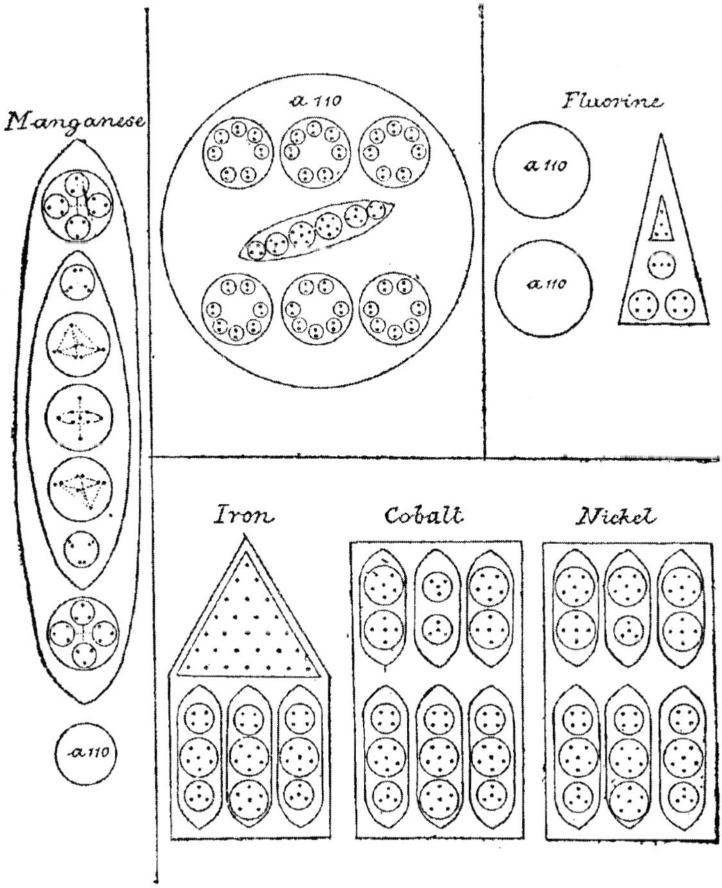

3 4 5

manganese are violently forced into company with which they have hardly any points of relationship, and that they intrude into an otherwise very harmonious group of closely similar composition. Moreover, manganese reproduces the characteristic lithium 'spike' and not the bars of those into whose company it is thrust, and it is thus allied with lithium, with which, indeed it is almost identical. But lithium is placed by Crookes at the head of a group, the other members of which are potassium, rubidium and cœsium (the last not examined). Following these identities of composition, I think it is better to remove manganese and fluorine from their incongruous companions, and place them with lithium and its allies as V *a*, the Spike Groups, marking, by the identity of number, similarities of arrangement which exist, and by the separation the differences of composition. It is worth while noting what Sir William Crookes, in his *Genesis of the Elements*, remarks on the relations of the inter-periodic group with its neighbors. He says: "These bodies are interperiodic because their atomic weights exclude them from the small periods into which the other elements fall, and because their chemical relations with some members of the neighboring groups show that they are probably interperiodic in the sense of being in transition stages."

Group V in every case shows fourteen bars radiating from a centre as shown in iron, Plate IV., 1 (opposite p. 14). While the form remains unchanged throughout, the increase of weight is gained by adding to the number of atoms contained in a bar. The group is made up, not of single chemical elements, as in all other cases, but of sub-groups, each containing three elements, and the relations within each sub-group are very close; moreover the weights only differ by two atoms per bar, making a weight difference of twenty-eight in the whole. Thus we have per bar:

Iron	72	Ruthenium	132	Osmium	245
Nickel	74	Rhodium	134	Iridium	247
Cobalt	76	Palladium	136	Platinum A	249
				Platinum B	257

It will be noticed (Plate XVII., 3,4,5,) that each bar has two sections, and that the three lower sections in iron, cobalt and nickel are identical; in the upper sections, iron has a cone of twenty-eight atoms, while cobalt and nickel have each three ovoids, and of these the middle ones alone differ, and that only in their upper globes, this globe being four-atomed in cobalt and six-atomed in nickel.

The long ovoids within each bar revolve round the central axis of the bar, remaining parallel with it, while each spins on its own axis ; the iron cone spins round as though impaled on the axis.

IRON. (Plate IV., 1, and XVII., 3).

14 bars of 72 atoms	...	1008
Atomic Weight	...	55·47
Number Weight $\frac{1008}{18}$	...	56·00

COBALT. (Plate XVII., 4).

14 bars of 74 atoms	...	1036
Atomic Weight	...	57·70
Number Weight $\frac{1036}{18}$	...	57·55

NICKEL. (Plate XVII., 4).

14 bars of 76 atoms	...	1064
Atomic Weight	...	58·30
Number Weight $\frac{1064}{18}$	...	59·11

(The weight of cobalt, as given in Erdmann's *Lehrbuch*, is 58·55, but Messrs. Parker & Sexton, in *Nature*, August 1, 1907, give the weight, as the result of their experiments, as 57·7.)

The next sub-group, ruthenium, rhodium, and palladium, has nothing to detain us. It will be observed that each bar contains eight segments, instead of the six of cobalt and nickel ; that ruthenium and palladium have the same number of atoms in their upper ovoids, although in ruthenium a triplet and quartet represent the septet of palladium ; and that in ruthenium and rhodium the lower ovoids are identical, though one has the order: sixteen, fourteen, sixteen, fourteen ; and the other : fourteen, sixteen, fourteen, sixteen. One constantly asks oneself : What is the significance of these minute changes ? Future investigators will probably discover the answer.

RUTHENIUM : (Plate XVIII., 1).

14 bars of 132 atoms	...	1848
Atomic Weight	...	100·91
Number Weight $\frac{1848}{18}$	...	102·66

RHODIUM : (Plate XVIII., 2).

14 bars of 134 atoms	...	1876
Atomic Weight	...	102·23
Number Weight $\frac{1876}{18}$	...	104·22

Plate XVIII.

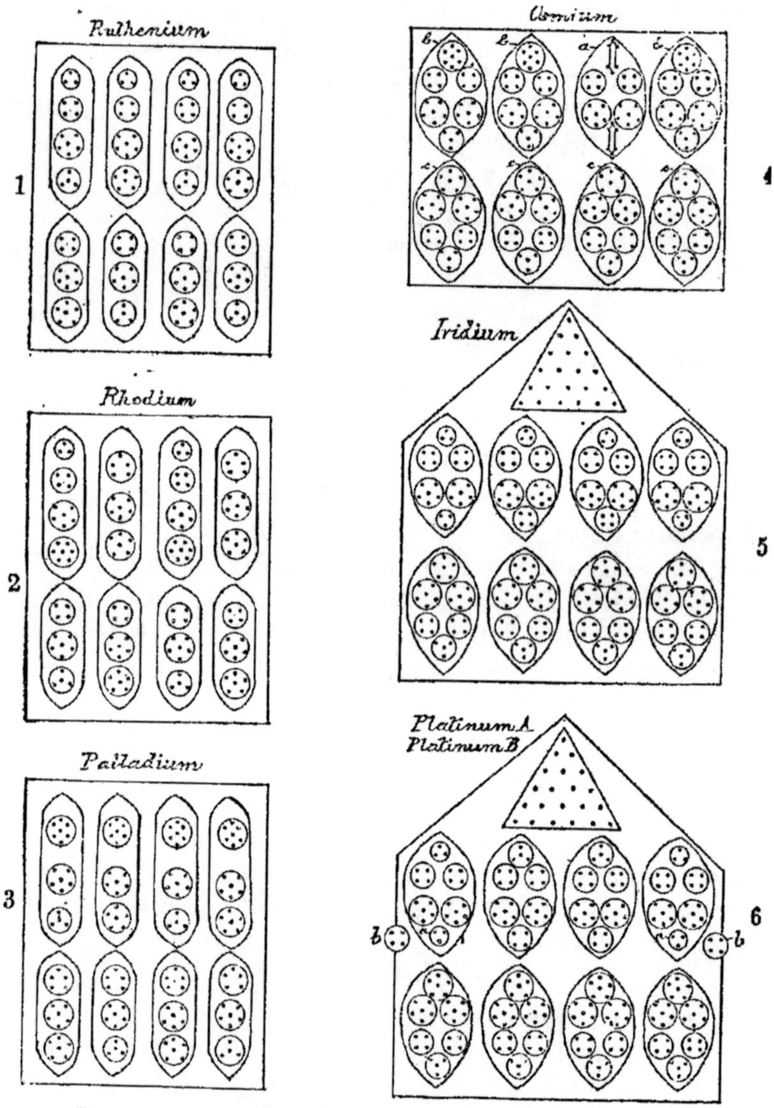

Palladium : (Plate XVIII., 3).

14 bars of 136 atoms	... 1904
Atomic Weight	... 105·74
Number Weight $\frac{1904}{18}$	... 105·77

The third sub-group, osmium, iridium and platinum, is, of course, more complicated in its composition, but its builders succeed in preserving the bar form, gaining the necessary increase by a multiplication of contained spheres within the ovoids. Osmium has one peculiarity: the ovoid marked *a* (Plate XVIII., 4) takes the place of axis in the upper half of the bar, and the three ovoids, marked *b*, revolve round it. In the lower half, the four ovoids, *c*, revolve round the central axis. In platinum, we have marked two forms as platinum A and platinum B, the latter having two four-atomed spheres (Plate XVIII., 6 *b*) in the place of the two triplets marked *a*. It may well be that what we have called platinum B is not a variety of platinum, but a new element, the addition of two atoms in a bar being exactly that which separates the other elements within each of the sub-groups. It will be noticed that the four lower sections of the bars are identical in all the members of this sub-group, each ovoid containing thirty atoms. The upper ring of ovoids in iridium and platinum A are also identical, but for the substitution, in platinum A, of a quartet for a triplet in the second and third ovoids; their cones are identical, containing twenty-one atoms, like those of silver and tin.

OSMIUM: (Plate XVIII., 4).

14 bars of 245 atoms	... 3430
Atomic Weight	... 189·55
Number Weight $\frac{3430}{18}$	... 190·55

IRIDIUM: (Plate XVIII., 5).

14 bars of 247 atoms	... 3458
Atomic Weight	... 191·11
Number Weight $\frac{3458}{18}$	... 192·11

PLATINUM A: (Plate XVIII., 6 *a*).

14 Bars of 249 atoms	... 3486
Atomic Weight	... 193·66
Number Weight $\frac{3486}{18}$	... 193·34

PLATINUM B: (Plate XVIII., 6 *b*).

14 bars of 251 atoms	... 3514
Atomic Weight	... ——
Number Weight $\frac{3574}{78}$	... 195·22

VA. THE SPIKE GROUPS.

I place within this group lithium, potassium, rubidium, fluorine, and manganese, because of their similarity in internal composition. Manganese has fourteen spikes, arranged as in the iron group, but radiating from a central globe. Potassium has nine, rubidium has sixteen, in both cases radiating from a central globe. Lithium (Plate IV., 2) and fluorine (Plate IV., 3) are the two types which dominate the group, lithium supplying the spike which is reproduced in all of them, and fluorine the 'nitrogen balloon' which appears in all save lithium. It will be seen that the natural affinities are strongly marked. They are all monads and paramagnetic ; lithium, potassium and rubidium are positive, while fluorine and manganese are negative. We seem thus to have a pair, corresponding with each other, as in other cases, and the interperiodic group is left interperiodic and congruous within itself.

LITHIUM (Plate IV., 2 and Plate XIX. 1) is a striking and beautiful form, with its upright cone, or spike, its eight radiating petals (*x*) at the base of the cone, and the plate-like support in the centre of which is a globe, on which the spike rests. The spike revolves swiftly on its axis, carrying the petals with it ; the plate revolves equally swiftly in the opposite direction. Within the spike are two globes and a long ovoid ; the spheres within the globe revolve as a cross ; within the ovoid are four spheres containing atoms arranged on tetrahedra, and a central sphere with an axis of three atoms surrounded by a spinning wheel of six.

LITHIUM :	Spike of 63 atoms	...	63
	8 petals of 6 atoms	...	48
	Central Globe of 16 atoms	...	16
	Total	...	127
	Atomic Weight	...	6·98
	Number Weight $\frac{127}{18}$	...	7·05

POTASSIUM (Plate 2 XIX.,) consists of nine radiating lithium spikes, but has no petals ; its central globe contains one hundred and thirty-four atoms, consisting of the 'nitrogen balloon', encircled by six four-atomed spheres,

PLATE XIX.

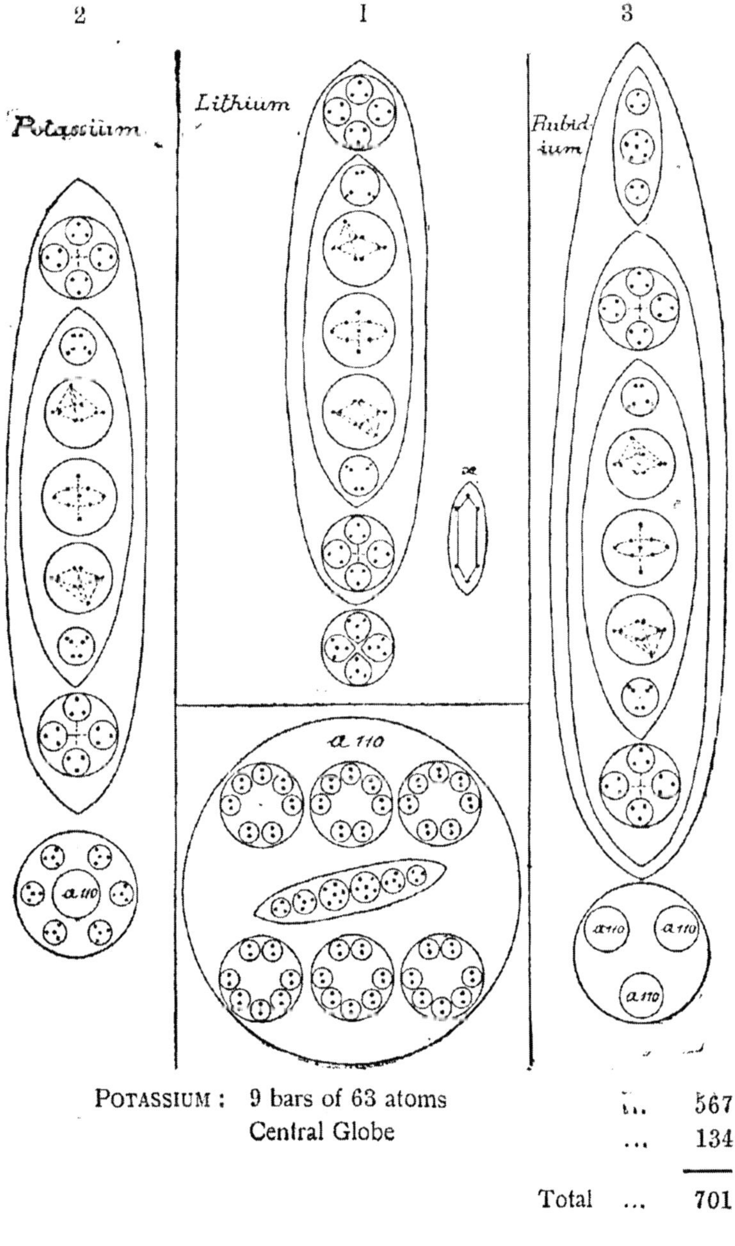

POTASSIUM :	9 bars of 63 atoms	...	567
	Central Globe	...	134
	Total	...	701

Atomic Weight	...	38·94
Number Weight $\frac{701}{18}$	...	38·85

(The weight, as determined by Richards [*Nature*, July 18, 1907] is 39·114.)

RUBIDIUM: (Plate XIX., 3) adds an ovoid, containing three spheres—two triplets and a sextet—to the lithium spike, of which it has sixteen, and its central globe is composed of three 'balloons.'

RUBIDIUM:	16 spikes of 75 atoms	...	1200
	Central Globe	...	330
	Total	...	1530
	Atomic Weight	...	84·85
	Number Weight $\frac{1530}{18}$	...	85·00

The corresponding negative group consists only of fluorine and manganese, so far as our investigations have gone.

FLUORINE (Plate IV., 3, and Plate XVII., 1) is a most peculiar looking object like a projectile, and gives one the impression of being ready to shoot off on the smallest provocation. The eight spikes, reversed funnels, coming to a point, are probably responsible for this warlike appearance. The remainder of the body is occupied by two 'balloons'.

FLUORINE:	8 spikes of 15 atoms	...	120
	2 balloons	...	220
	Total	...	340
	Atomic Weight	...	18·90
	Number Weight $\frac{340}{18}$	...	18·88

MANGANESE (Plate XVII., 2) has fourteen spikes radiating from a central 'balloon.'

MANGANESE:	14 spikes of 63 atoms	...	882
	Central Balloon	...	110
	Total	...	992
	Atomic Weight	...	54·57
	Number Weight $\frac{992}{18}$	...	55·11

X.

We have now to consider the breaking up of the octohedral groups, and more and more, as we proceed, do we find that the most complicated arrangements are reducible to simple elements which are already familiar.

CARBON (PLATE III., 5 and XV., 1).

Carbon is the typical octohedron, and a clear understanding of this will enable us to follow easily the constitution and disintegra-

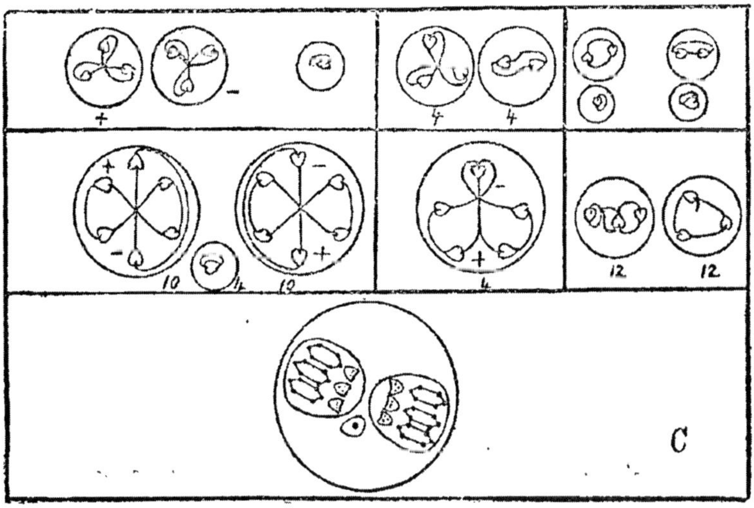

tion of the various members of these groups. Its appearance as a chemical atom is shown on Plate III. (opposite p. 14, and see Plate XV. 1, 64). On the proto level the chemical atom breaks up into four segments, each consisting of a pair of funnels connected by a single atom; this is the proto element which appears at the end of each arm of the cross in titanium and zirconium. On the meta level the five six-atomed 'cigars' show two neutral combinations, and the truncated 'cigar' of five atoms is also neutral; the 'leaves' yield two forms of triplet, five different types being thus yielded by each pair of funnels, exclusive of the linking atom. The hyper level has triplets, duads and units.

TITANIUM (PLATE III., 6 and XV., 2, 3).

On the proto level, the cross breaks up completely, setting free the pairs of funnels with the linking atom (*a* and *b*), as in carbon,

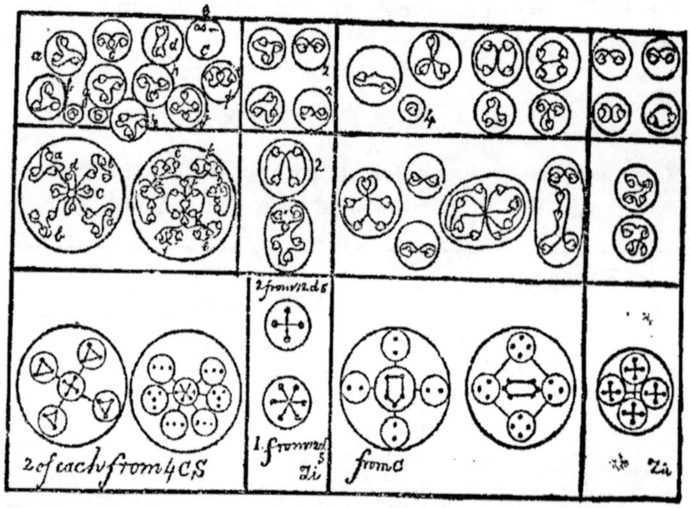

the four bodies marked *c*, the twelve marked *d*, and the central globe marked *e*. The latter breaks up again, setting free its five intersecting cigar-bearing tetrahedra, which follow their usual course (see Occultum, p. 28). The eight-atomed body in the centre makes a ring of seven atoms round a central one, like that in occultum (see p. 28, diagram B), from which it only differs in having the central atom, and breaks up similarly, setting the central atom free. The ovoid *c* sets free its four contained globes, and the ovoid *d* sets free the three within it. Thus sixty-one proto elements are yielded by titanium. On the meta level, *c* (titanium 3) breaks up into star-like and cruciform bodies ; the component parts of these are easily followed ; on the hyper level, of the four forms of triplets one behaves as in carbon, and the others are shown, *a*, *b* and *f* ; the cruciform quintet yields a triplet and a duad, *c* and *d* ; the tetrahedra yield two triplets *g* and *h*, and two units ; the septet, a triplet *k* and a quartet *j*. On the meta level, the bodies from *d* behave like their equivalents in sodium, each *d* shows two quartets and a sextet, breaking up, on the hyper level, into four duads and two triads.

Zirconium (Plate XV., 2, 5).

Zirconium reproduces in its *c* the four forms that we have already followed in the corresponding *c* of titanium, and as these are set free on the proto level, and follow the same course on the meta and hyper levels, we need not repeat them. The central globe of zirconium *c* sets free its nine contained bodies ; eight of these are similar and are figured in the diagram ; it will be observed that the central body is the truncated 'cigar' of carbon ; their behavior on the meta and hyper levels is easily followed there. The central sphere is also figured ; the cigar follows its usual course, and its companions unite into a sextet and an octet. The *d* ovoid liberates five bodies, four of which we have already seen in titanium, as the crosses and sextet of sodium, and which are figured under titanium ; the four quartets within the larger globe also follow a sodium model, and are given again.

Silicon (Plate XVI., 1).

In Silicon, the ovoids are set free from the funnels on the proto level, and the truncated 'cigar,' playing the part of a leaf, is also liberated. This, and the four 'cigars,' which escape from their ovoids, pass along their usual course. The quintet and quartet remain together, and form a nine-atomed body on the meta level, yielding a sextet and a triplet on the hyper.

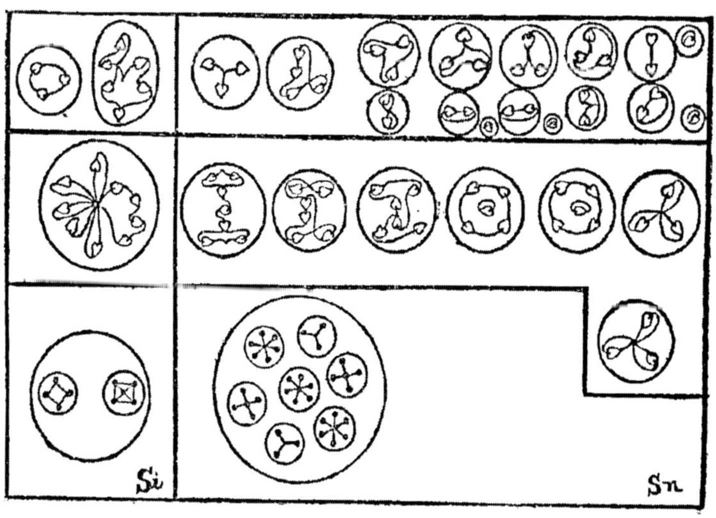

Germanium (Plate XVI., 2, 4).

The central globe, with its two 'cigar'-bearing tetrahedra, need not delay us ; the tetrahedra are set free and follow the occultum disintegration, and the central four atoms is the sodium cross that we had in titanium. The ovoids (XVI., 4) are liberated on the proto level, and the 'cigar,' as usual, bursts its way through and goes along its accustomed path. The others remain linked on the meta level, and break up into two triangles and a quintet on the hyper.

Tin (Plate XVI., 3, 4).

Here we have only the spike to consider, as the funnels are the same as in germanium, and the central globe is that of titanium, omitting the eight-atomed centre. The cone of the spike we have had in silver (see p. 729, May), and it is set free on the proto level. The spike, as in zinc, becomes a large sphere, with the single septet in the centre, the remaining six bodies circling round it on differing planes. They break up as shown. (Tin is Sn.)

Iron (Plate IV., 1., and XVII., 3).

We have already dealt with the affinities of this peculiar group, and we shall see, in the disintegration, even more clearly, the close relationships which exist according to the classification which we here follow.

The fourteen bars of iron break asunder on the proto level, and each sets free its contents—a cone and three ovoids, which as usual, become spheres. The twenty-eight-atomed cone becomes a four-sided figure, and the ovoids show crystalline contents. They break up, on the meta level as shown in the diagram, and are all reduced to triplets and duads on the hyper level.

Cobalt (Plate XVII., 4).

The ovoids in cobalt are identical with those of iron ; the higher ovoids, which replace the cone of iron, show persistently the crystalline forms so noticeable throughout this group.

Nickel (Plate XVII., 5).

The two additional atoms in a bar, which alone separate nickel from cobalt, are seen in the upper sphere of the central ovoid.

RUTHENIUM (PLATE XVIII., 1).

The lower ovoids in ruthenium are identical in composition with those of iron, cobalt and nickel and may be studied under iron. The upper ones only differ by the addition of a triplet.

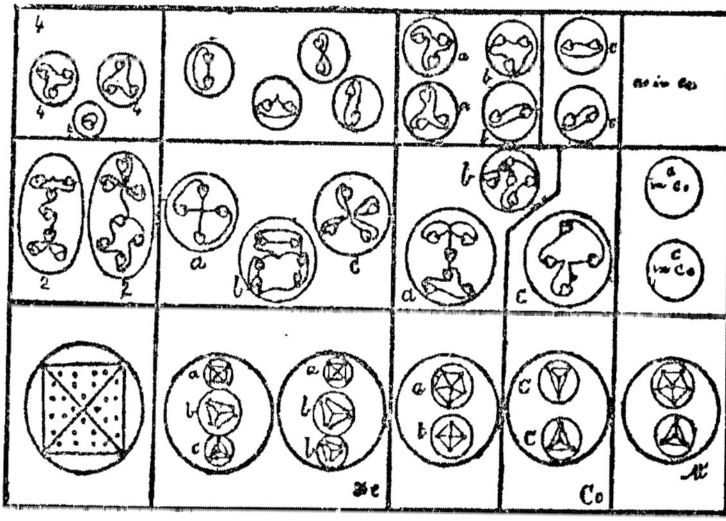

RHODIUM (PLATE XVIII., 2).

Rhodium has a septet, which is to be seen in the *c* of titannium (see *k* in the titanium diagram above) and differs only in this from its group.

PALLADIUM (PLATE XVIII., 3).

In palladium this septet appears as the upper sphere in every ovoid of the upper ring.

OSMIUM (PLATE XVIII., 4).

We have here no new constituents ; the ovoids are set free on the proto level and the contained globes on the meta, all being of familiar forms. The cigars, as usual, break free on the proto level, and leave their ovoid with only four contained spheres, which unite into two nine-atomed bodies as in silicon, (see above).

IRIDIUM (PLATE XVIII., 5).

The twenty-one atomed cone of silver here re-appears, and its proceedings may be followed under that metal (see diagram, p. 729, May). The remaining bodies call for no remark.

PLATINUM (PLATE XVIII., 6).

Again the silver cone is with us. The remaining bodies are set free on the proto level, and their contained spheres on the meta.

LITHIUM (PLATE IV., 2, and XIX., 1).

Here we have some new combinations, which recur persistently in its allies. The bodies *a*, in Plate XIX., 1, are at the top and bottom of the ellipse ; they come to right and left of it in the proto state, and each makes a twelve-atomed body on the meta level.

The five bodies within the ellipse, three monads and two sextets, show two which we have had before : *d*, which behaves like the quintet and quartet in silicon, after their junction, and *b*, which we have had in iron. The two bodies *c* are a variant of the square-based pyramid, one atom at the apex, and two at each of the other angles. The globe, *e*, is a new form, the four tetrahedra of the proto level making a single twelve-atomed one on the meta. The body *a* splits up into triplets on the hyper ; *b* and *d* follow their iron and silicon models ; *d* yields four duads and a unit ; *e* breaks into four quartets.

POTASSIUM (PLATE XIX., 2).

Potassium repeats the lithium spike ; the central globe shows the 'nitrogen balloon,' which we already know, and which is surrounded

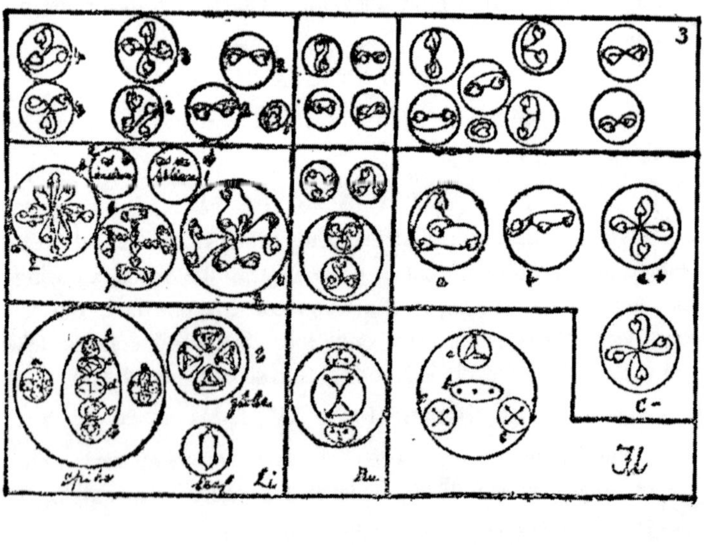

on the proto level with six tetrahedra, which are set free on the meta and behave as in cobalt. Hence we have nothing new.

RUBIDIUM (PLATE XIX., 3).

Again the lithium spike, modified slightly by the introduction of an ovoid, in place of the top sphere ; the forms here are somewhat unusual, and the triangles of the sextet revolve round each other on the meta level ; all the triads break up on the hyper level into duads and units.

FLUORINE (PLATE IV., 3, AND PLATE XVII., 1):

The reversed funnels of fluorine split asunder on the proto level, and are set free, the 'balloons' also floating off independently. The funnels, as usual, become spheres, and on the meta level set free their contained bodies, three quartets and a triplet from each of the eight. The balloons disintegrate in the usual way.

MANGANESE (PLATE XVII., 2).

Manganese offers us nothing new, being composed of 'lithium spikes' and 'nitrogen balloons.'

XI.

VI. THE STAR GROUPS.

We have now reached the last of the groups, as arranged on Sir William Crookes' lemniscates, that forming the 'neutral column ; it is headed by helium, which is *sui generis.* The remainder are in the form of a flat star (see Plate IV., 4), with a centre formed of five intersecting and 'cigar'-bearing tetrahedra, and six radiating arms. Ten of these have been observed, five pairs in which the second member differs but slightly from the first ; they are : Neon, Meta-neon ; Argon, Metargon ; Krypton, Meta-krypton ; Xenon, Meta-xenon ; Kalon, Meta-kalon ; the last pair and the meta forms are not yet discovered by chemists. These all show the presence of a periodic law ; taking an arm of the star in each of the five pairs, we find the number of atoms to be as follows :

40	99	224	363	489
47	106	231	370	496

It will be observed that the meta form, in each case shows seven more atoms than its fellow.

HELIUM (Plate III., 5, and Plate XX., 1), shows two 'cigar'-bearing tetrahedra, and two hydrogen triangles, the tetrahedra revolving round an egg-shaped central body, and the triangles spinning on their own axes while performing a similar revolution. The whole has an attractively airy appearance, as of a fairy element.

HELIUM :	Two tetrahedra of 24 atoms	...	48
	Two triangles of 9 atoms	...	18
	Central egg	...	6
	Total	...	72
	Atomic Weight	...	3·94
	Number Weight $\frac{72}{18}$	...	4·00

NEON (Plate XX., 2 and 6) has six arms of the pattern shown in 2, radiating from the central globe.

NEON :	Six arms of 40 atoms	...	240
	Central tetrahedra	...	120
	Total	...	360
	Atomic Weight	...	19·90
	Number Weight $\frac{360}{18}$	...	20·00

PLATE XX.

META-NEON (Plate XX., 3 and 6) differs from its comrade by the insertion of an additional atom in each of the groups included in the second body within its arm, and substituting a seven-atomed group for one of the triplets in neon.

META-NEON :	Six arms of 47 atoms	...	282
	Central tetrahedra	...	120
	Total	...	402
	Atomic Weight	...	—
	Number Weight $\frac{402}{18}$	...	22·33

ARGON (Plate XX., 4, 6 and 7) shows within its arms the *b* 63 which we met in nitrogen, yttrium, vanadium and niobium, but not the 'balloon,' which we shall find with it in krypton and its congeners.

PLATE XX.

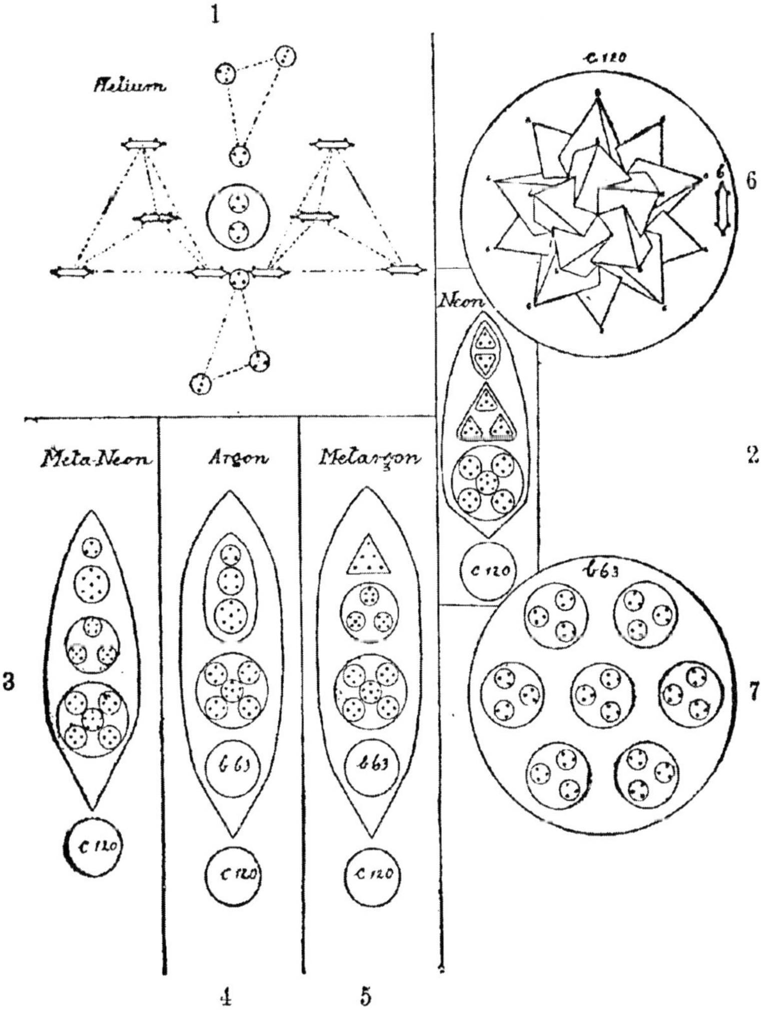

ARGON : Six arms of 99 atoms	...	594
Central tetrahedra	...	120
Total	...	714
Atomic Weight	...	39·60
Number Weight $\frac{714}{18}$	...	39·66

METARGON (Plate XX., 5, 6 and 7) again shows only an additional seven atoms in each arm.

METARGON :	Six arms of 106 atoms	...	636
	Central tetrahedra	...	120
	Total	...	756
	Atomic Weight	...	—
	Number Weight $\frac{756}{18}$	...	42

KRYPTON (Plate XXI., 1 and 4, and Plate XX, 6 and 7) contains the nitrogen ' balloon,' elongated by its juxtaposition to *b* 63. The central tetrahedra appear as usual.

KRYPTON :	Six arms of 224 atoms	...	1344
	Central tetrahedra	...	120
	Total	...	1464
	Atomic Weight	...	81·20
	Number Weight $\frac{1464}{18}$	...	81·33

META-KRYPTON differs only from krypton by the substitution of *z* for *y* in each arm of the star.

META-KRYPTON :	Six arms of 231 atoms	...	1386
	Central tetrahedra	...	120
	Total	...	1506
	Atomic Weight	...	—
	Number Weight $\frac{1506}{18}$	...	83·66

PLATE XXI.

ZENON (Plate XXI., 2 and 4, and Plate XX 6 and 7) has a peculiarity shared only by kalon, that *x* and *y* are asymmetrical, the centre of one having three atoms and the centre of the other two. Is this done in order to preserve the difference of seven from its comrade ?

ZENON :	Six arms of 363 atoms	...	2178
	Central tetrahedra	...	120
	Total	...	2298
	Atomic Weight	...	127·10
	Number Weight $\frac{2298}{18}$	...	127·66

PLATE XXI.

1

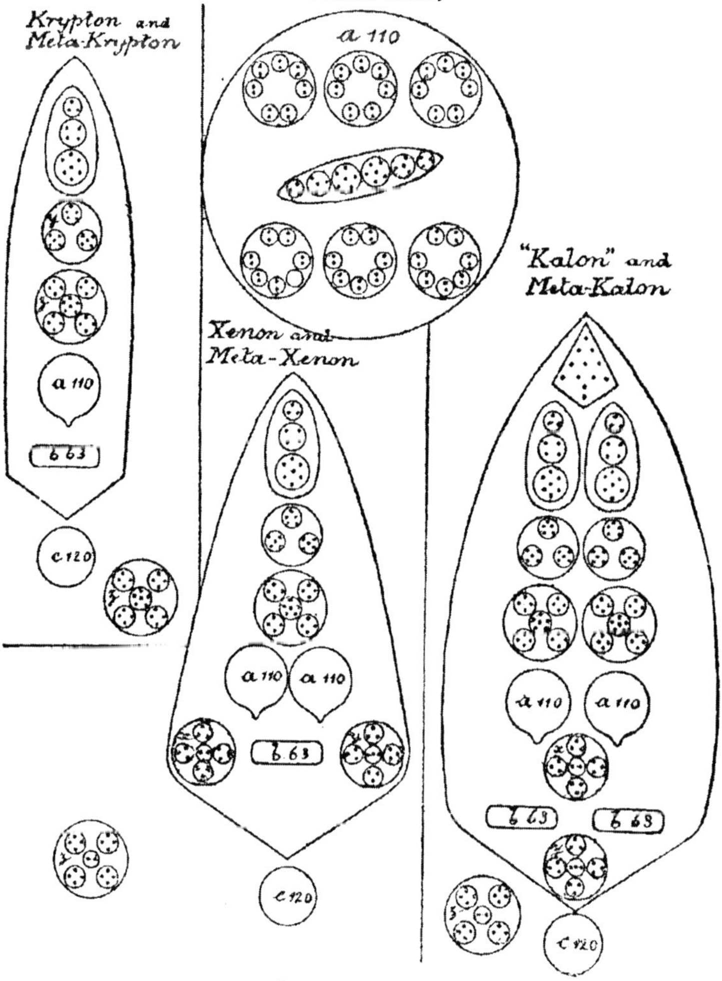

2

META-ZENON differs from zenon only by the substitution of two *z*s for *x* and *y*.

META-ZENON :	Six arms of 370 atoms	...	2220
	Central tetrahedra	...	120
	Total	...	2340
	Atomic Weight	...	
	Number Weight $\frac{2340}{18}$	...	169·66

KALON (Plate XXI., 3 and 4, and Plate XX., 6 and 7) has a curious cone, possessing a kind of tail which we have not observed elsewhere ; *x* and *y* show the same asymmetry as in zenon.

KALON :	Six arms of 489 atoms	...	2934
	Central tetrahedra	...	120
	Total	...	3054
	Atomic Weight	...	—
	Number Weight $\frac{3054}{18}$	...	169·66

META-KALON again substitutes 2 *zs* for *x* and *y*.

META-KALON :	Six arms of 496 atoms	...	2976
	Central tetrahedra	...	120
	Total	...	3096
	Atomic Weight	...	—
	Number Weight $\frac{3096}{18}$	...	172

Only a few atoms of kalon and meta-kalon have been found in the air of a fair-sized room.

It does not seem worth while to break up these elements, for their component parts are so familiar. The complicated groups—*a* 110, *b* 63 and *c* 120—have all been fully dealt with in preceding pages.

There remains now only Radium, of the elements which we have, so far, examined, and that will be now described and will bring to an end this series of observations. A piece of close and detailed work of this kind, although necessarily imperfect, will have its value in the future, when science along its own lines shall have confirmed these researches.

It will have been observed that our weights, obtained by counting, are almost invariably slightly in excess of the orthodox ones : it is interesting that in the latest report of the International Commission (November 13, 1907), printed in the *Proceedings of the Chemical Society of London*, Vol. XXIV, No. 33, and issued on January 25, 1908, the weight of hydrogen is now taken at 1·008 instead of at 1. This would slightly raise all the orthodox weights ; thus aluminium rises from 26·91 to 27·1, antimony from 119·34 to 120·2, and so on.

XII.

Radium.

Radium has the form of a tetrahedron, and it is in the tetrahedral groups (see article V) that we shall find its nearest congeners; calcium, strontium, chromium, molybdenum resemble it most closely in general internal arrangements, with additions from zinc and cadmium. Radium has a complex central sphere (Plate XXII), extraordinarily vivid and living; the whirling motion is so rapid that continued accurate observation is very difficult; the sphere is more closely compacted than the centre-piece in other elements, and is much larger in proportion to the funnels and spikes than is the case with the elements above named; reference to Plate VIII will show that in these the funnels are much

PLATE XXII.

Radium—centre 819 atoms

larger than the centres, whereas in radium the diameter of the sphere and the length of the funnel or spike are about equal. Its heart consists of a globe containing seven atoms, which assume on the proto level the prismatic form shown in cadmium, magnesium and selenium. This globe is the centre of two crosses, the arms of which show respectively three-atomed and two-atomed groups. Round this sphere are arranged, as on radii, twenty-four segments, each containing five bodies—four quintets and a septet—and six loose atoms, which float horizontally across the mouth of the segment; the whole sphere has thus a kind of surface of atoms. On the proto level these six atoms in each segment gather together and form a 'cigar.' In the rush of the streams

PLATE XXIII.

Radium-funnel 618 atoms

presently to be described one of these atoms is occasionally torn away, but is generally, if not always, replaced by the capture of another which is flung into the vacated space.

Each of the four funnels opens, as usual, on one face of the tetrahedron, and they resemble the funnels of strontium and molybdenum but contain three pillars instead of four (Plate XXIII). They stand within the funnel as though at the angles of a triangle, not side by side. The contained bodies, though numerous, contain forms which are all familiar.

The spikes alternate with the funnels, and point to the angles of the tetrahedron as in zinc and cadmium ; each spike contains three 'lithium spikes' (see Plate XIX) with a ten-atomed cone or cap at the top, floating above the three (Plate XXIV). The 'petals' 'or cigars' of lithium exist in the central globe in the floating atoms, and the four-atomed groups which form the lithium 'plate' may be seen in the funnels, so that the whole of lithium appears in radium.

So much for its composition. But a very peculiar result, so far unobserved elsewhere, arises from the extraordinarily rapid whirling of the central sphere. A kind of vortex is formed, and there is a constant and powerful indraught through the funnels. By this, particles are drawn in from without, and these are swept round with the sphere, their temperature becoming much raised, and they are then violently shot out though the spikes. It is these jets which occasionally sweep away an atom from the surface of the sphere. These 'particles' may be atoms, or they may be bodies from any of the etheric levels ; in some cases these bodies break up and form new combinations. In fact lithium seems like a kind of vortex of creative activity, drawing in, breaking up, recombining, shooting forth—a most extraordinary element.

LITHIUM :	4 funnels of 618 atoms	2472
	4 spikes of 199 atoms	796
	Central sphere	819
	Total...	4087
	Atomic weight	
	Number weight $\frac{4087}{18}$	227·05

PLATE XXIV.

Radium – spike 199 atoms

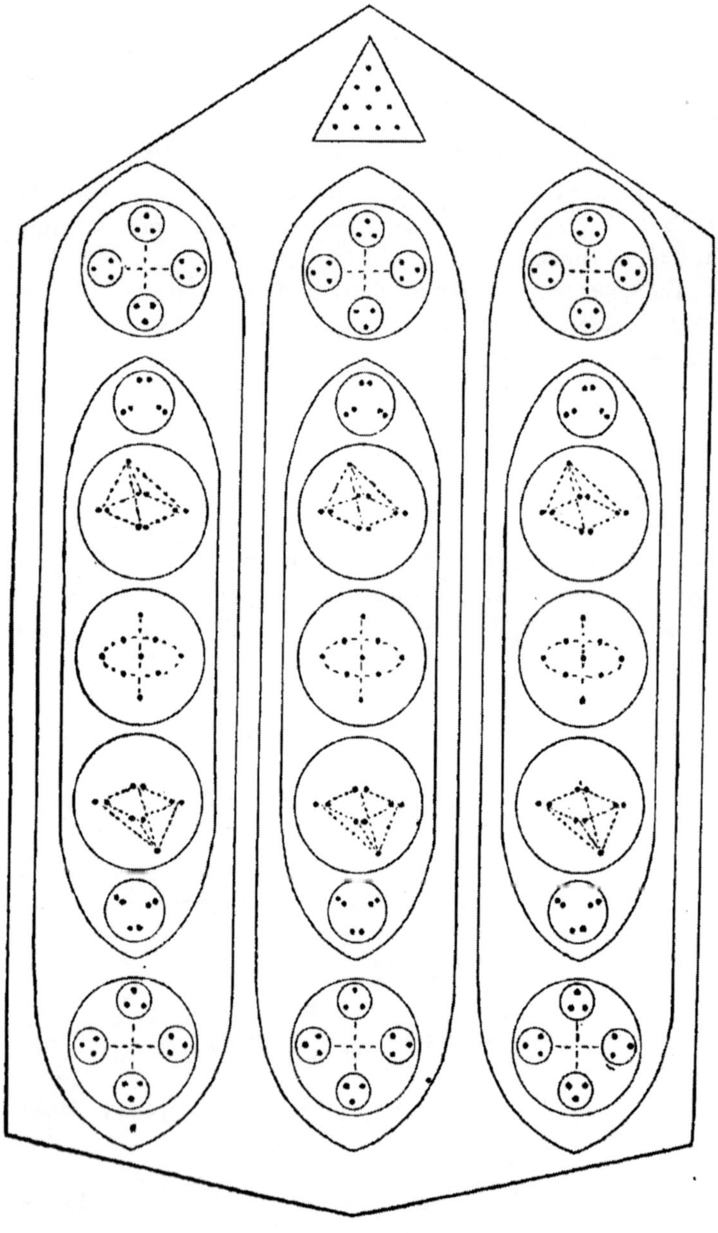

APPENDIX.

THE ÆTHER OF SPACE.

Much discussion has taken place, especially between physicists and chemists, over the nature of the substances with which all space must, according to scientific hypothesis, be filled. One side contends that it is infinitely thinner than the thinnest gas, absolutely frictionless and without weight; the other asserts that it is denser than the densest solid. In this substance the ultimate atoms of matter are thought to float, like motes in a sunbeam, and light, heat and electricity are supposed to be its vibrations.

Theosophical investigators, using methods not at the disposal of physical science, have found that this hypothesis includes under one head two entirely different and widely separated sets of phenomena. They have been able to deal with states of matter higher than the gaseous and have observed that it is by means of vibrations of this finer matter that light, heat and electricity manifest themselves to us. Seeing that matter in these higher states thus performs the functions attributed to the ether of science, they have (perhaps unadvisedly) called these states etheric, and have thus left themselves without a convenient name for that substance which fulfils the other part of the scientific requirements.

Let us for the moment name this substance *koilon*, since it fills what we are in the habit of calling empty space. What mūlaprakṛṭi, or 'mother-matter,' is to the inconceivable totality of universes, koilon is to our particular universe—not to our solar system merely but to the vast unit which includes all visible suns. Between koilon and mūlaprakṛṭi there must be various stages, but we have at present no direct means of estimating their number or of knowing anything whatever about them.

In an ancient occult treatise, however, we read of a "colorless spiritual fluid" "which exists everywhere and forms the first foundation on which our solar system is built. Outside the latter, it is found in its pristine pŭrity only between the stars [suns] of the universe. . . . As its substance is of a different kind from that known on earth, the inhabitants of the latter, seeing *through it*, believe, in their illusion and ignorance, that it is empty space. There is not one finger's breadth of void space in the whole boundless universe."* "The mother-substance" is said, in this treatise, to produce this æther of space as its seventh grade of density, and all objective suns are said to have this for their 'substance.'

To any power of sight which we can bring to bear upon it, this koilon appears to be homogeneous, though it is probably nothing of the kind, since homogeneity can belong to the mother-substance alone. It is out of all proportion denser than any other substance known to us, infinitely denser—if we may be pardoned the expression; so much denser that it seems to belong to another type, or order, of density. But now comes the startling part of the investigation: we might expect matter to be a densification of this koilon; it is nothing of the kind. Matter is not koilon, but *the absence of koilon*, and at first sight, matter and space appear to have changed places, and emptiness has become solidity, solidity has become emptiness.

To help us to understand this clearly let us examine the ultimate atom of the physical plane, (see pp. 5-7). It is composed of ten rings or wires, which lie side by side, but never touch one another. If one of these wires be taken away from the atom, and be, as it were, untwisted from its peculiar spiral shape and laid out on a flat surface, it will be seen that it is a complete circle—a tightly twisted endless coil. This coil is itself a spiral containing 1680 turns; it can be unwound, and it will then make a much larger circle. This process of unwinding may be again performed, and a still bigger circle obtained, and this can be repeated till the seven sets of spirillæ are all unwound, and we have a huge circle of the tiniest imaginable dots, like pearls threaded on an invisible string. These dots are so inconceivably small that many millions of them are needed to make one ultimate physical atom, and while the exact number is not readily ascertainable, several different lines of calculation agree in indicating it as closely approximate to the almost inconceivable total of fourteen thousand millions. Where figures are so huge, direct counting is obviously impossible, but fortunately the different parts of the atom are sufficiently alike to enable us to make an estimate in which the margin of error is not likely to be very

* Quoted in *The Secret Doctrine.* H.P. Blavatsky, i. 309.

great. The atom consists of ten wires, which divide themselves naturally into two groups—the three which are thicker and more prominent, and the seven thinner ones which correspond to the colors and planets. These latter appear to be identical in constitution though the forces flowing through them must differ, since each responds most readily to its own special set of vibrations. By actual counting it has been discovered that the numbers of coils or spirillæ of the first order in each wire is 1680; and the proportion of the different orders of spirillæ to one another is equal in all cases that have been examined, and correspond with the number of dots in the ultimate spirillæ of the lowest order. The ordinary sevenfold rule works quite accurately with the thinner coils, but there is a very curious variation with regard to the set of three. As may be seen from the drawings, these are obviously thicker and more prominent, and this increase of size is produced by an augmentation (so slight as to be barely perceptible) in the proportion to one another of the different orders of spirillæ and in the number of dots in the lowest. This augmentation, amounting at present to not more than ·00571428 of the whole in each case, suggests the unexpected possibility that this portion of the atom may be somehow actually undergoing a change—may in fact be in process of growth, as there is reason to suppose that these three thicker spirals originally resembled the others.

Since observation shows us that each physical atom is represented by forty-nine astral atoms, each astral atom by forty-nine mental atoms, and each mental atom by forty-nine of those on the buddhic plane, we have here evidently several terms of a regular progressive series, and the natural presumption is that the series continues where we are no longer able to observe it. Further probability is lent to this assumption by the remarkable fact that—if we assume one dot to be what corresponds to an atom on the seventh or highest of our planes (as is suggested in *The Ancient Wisdom*, p. 42) and then suppose the law of multiplication to begin its operation, so that 49 dots shall form the atom of the next or sixth plane, 2401 that of the fifth, and so on—we find that the number indicated for the physical atom (49^6) corresponds almost exactly with the calculation based upon the actual counting of the coils. Indeed, it seems probable that but for the slight growth of the three thicker wires of the atom the correspondence would have been perfect.

It must be noted that a physical atom cannot be directly broken up into astral atoms. If the unit of force which whirls those millions of dots into the complicated shape of a physical atom be pressed back by an effort of will over the threshold of the astral plane, the atom disappears instantly, for the dots are released. But the same unit of force, working now upon a higher level, express itself not through one astral atom, but through a group of 49. If the process of pressing back the unit of force is repeated, so that it energises upon the mental plane, we find the group there enlarged to the number of 2401 of those higher atoms. Upon the buḍḍhic plane the number of atoms formed by the same amount of force is very much greater still—probably the cube of 49 instead of the square, though they have not been actually counted. Therefore one physical atom is not *composed of* forty-nine astral or 2401 mental atoms, but *corresponds* to them, in the sense that the force which manifests through it would show itself on those higher planes by energising respectively those numbers of atoms.

The dots, or beads, seem to be the constituents of all matter of which we, at present, know anything; astral, mental and buḍḍhic atoms are built of them, so we may fairly regard them as fundamental units, the basis of matter.

These units are all alike, spherical and absolutely simple in construction. Though they are the basis of all matter, they are not themselves matter; they are not blocks but bubbles. They do not resemble bubbles floating in the air, which consist of a thin film of water separating the air within them from the air outside, so that the film has both an outer and an inner surface. Their analogy is rather with the bubbles that we see rising in water, before they reach the surface, bubbles which may be said to have only one surface—that of the water which is pushed back by the contained air. Just as such bubbles are not water, but are precisely the spots from which water is absent, so these units are not koilon, but the absence of koilon—the only spots where it is not—specks of nothingness floating in it, so to speak, for the interior of these space-bubbles is an absolute void to the highest power of vision that we can turn upon them.

That is the startling, well-nigh incredible, fact. Matter is nothingness, the spaces obtained by pressing back an infinitely dense substance; Fohat "digs holes in space" of a verity, and the holes are the airy nothingnesses, the bubbles, of which 'solid' universes are built.

What are they, then, these bubbles, or rather, what is their content, the force which can blow bubbles in a substance of infinite density? The ancients called that force 'the Breath,' a graphic symbol, which seems to imply that they who used it had seen the kosmic process, had seen the LOGOS when He breathed into the 'waters of space,' and made the bubbles which build universes. Scientists may call this 'Force' by what names they will—names are nothing; to us, Theosophists, it is the Breath of the LOGOS, we know not whether of the LOGOS of this solar system or of a yet mightier Being; the latter would seem the more likely, since in the above-quoted occult treatise all visible suns are said to have this as their substance.

The Breath of the LOGOS, then, is the force which fills these spaces; His the force which holds them open against the tremendous pressure of the koilon; they are full of His Life, of Himself, and everything we call matter, on however high or low a plane, is instinct with divinity; these units of force, of life, the bricks with which He builds His universe, are His very life scattered through space; truly is it written: "I established this universe with a portion of myself." And when He draws in His breath, the waters of space will close in again, and the universe will have disappeared. It is only a breath.

The outbreathing which makes these bubbles is quite distinct from, and long antecedent to, the three outpourings, or Life-Waves, so familiar to the theosophical student. The first Life-Wave catches up these bubbles, and whirls them into the various arrangements which we call the atoms of the several planes, and aggregates them into the molecules, and, on the physical plane into the chemical elements. The worlds are built out of these voids, these emptinesses, which seem to us 'nothing' but are divine force. It is matter made from the privation of matter. How true were H. P. B.'s statements in *The Secret Doctrine*: "Matter is nothing but an aggregation of atomic forces" (iii. 398); Buḍḍha taught that the primitive substance is eternal and unchangeable. Its vehicle is the pure luminous æther, the boundless infinite space, not a void, resulting from the absence of all forms, but on the contrary, the foundation of all forms" (iii, 402).

How vividly, how unmistakably this knowledge brings home to us the great doctrine of Māyā, the transitoriness and unreality of earthly things, the utterly deceptive nature of appearances! When the candidate for initiation sees (not merely believes, remember, but actually *sees*) that what has always before seemed to him empty space is in reality a solid mass of inconceivable density, and that the matter which has appeared to be the one tangible and certain basis of things is not only by comparison tenuous as gossamer (the 'web' spun by 'Father-Mother'), but is actually composed of emptiness and nothingness—is itself the very negation of matter—then for the first time he thoroughly appreciates the valuelessness of the physical senses as guides to the truth. Yet even more clearly still stands out the glorious certainty of the immanence of the Divine; not only is everything ensouled by the LOGOS, but even its visible manifestation is literally part of Him, is built of His very substance, so that Matter as well as Spirit becomes sacred to the student who really understands.

The koilon in which all these bubbles are formed undoubtedly represents a part, and perhaps the principal part, of what science describes as the luminiferous æther. Whether it is actually the bearer of the vibrations of light and heat through interplanetary space is as yet undetermined. It is certain that these vibrations impinge upon and are perceptible to our bodily senses only through the etheric matter of the physical plane. But this by no means proves that they are conveyed through space in the same manner, for we know very little of the extent to which the physical etheric matter exists in interplanetary and interstellar space, though the examination of meteoric matter and kosmic dust shows that at least some of it is scattered there.

The scientific theory is that the æther has some quality which enables it to transmit at a certain definite velocity transverse waves of all lengths and intensities—that velocity being what is commonly called the speed of light, 190,000 miles per second. Quite probably this may be true of koilon, and if so it must also be capable of communicating those waves to bubbles or aggregations of bubbles, and before the light can reach our eyes there must be a downward transference from plane to plane similar to that taking place when a thought awakens emotion or causes action.

In a recent pamphlet on *The Density of Æther*, Sir Oliver Lodge remarks :

" Just as the ratio of mass to volume is small in the case of a solar system or a nebula or a cobweb, I have been driven to think that the observed mechanical density of matter is probably an excessively small fraction of the total density of the substance, or æther, contained in the space which it thus partially occupies—the substance of which it may hypothetically be held to be composed.

" Thus for instance, consider a mass of platinum, and assume that its atoms are composed of electrons, or of some structures not wholly dissimilar : the space which these bodies actually fill, as compared with the whole space which in a sense they 'occupy,' is comparable to one ten-millionth of the whole, even inside each atom ; and the fraction is still smaller if it refers to the visible mass. So that a kind of minimum estimate of ætherial density, on this basis, would be something like ten thousand million times that of platinum."

And further on he adds that this density may well turn out to be fifty thousand million times that of platinum. " The densest matter known," he says, " is trivial and gossamer-like compared with the unmodified æther in the same space."

Incredible as this seems to our ordinary ideas, it is undoubtedly an understatement rather than an exaggeration of the true proportion as observed in the case of koilon. We shall understand how this can be so if we remember that koilon seems absolutely homogeneous and solid even when examined by a power of magnification which makes physical atoms appear in size and arrangement like cottages scattered over a lonely moor, and when we further add to this the recollection that the bubbles of which these atoms in turn are composed are themselves what may be not inaptly called fragments of nothingness.

In the same pamphlet Sir Oliver Lodge makes a very striking estimate of the intrinsic energy of the æther. He says : " The total output of a million-kilowatt power station for thirty million years exists permanently, and at present inaccessibly, in every cubic millimetre of space." Here again he is probably underestimating rather than overestimating the stupendous truth.

It may naturally be asked how, if all this be so, it is possible that we can move about freely in a solid ten thousand million times denser, as Sir Oliver Lodge says, than platinum. The obvious answer is that, where densities differ sufficiently, they can move through each other with perfect freedom; water or air can pass through cloth; air can pass through water; an astral form passes unconsciously through a physical wall, or through an ordinary human, body; many of us have seen an astral form walk through a physical neither being conscious of the passage; it does not matter whether we say that a ghost has passed through a wall, or a wall has passed through a ghost. A gnome passes freely through a rock, and walks about within the earth, as comfortably as we walk about in the air. A deeper answer is that consciousness can recognise only consciousness, that since we are of the nature of the LOGOS we can sense only those things which are also of His nature. These bubbles are His essence, His life, and, therefore, we, who also are part of Him, can see the matter which is built of His substance, for all forms are but manifestations of Him. The koilon is to us non-manifestation, because we have not unfolded powers which enable us to cognise it, and it may be the manifestation of a loftier order of LOGOI, utterly beyond our ken.

As none of our investigators can raise his conciousness to the highest plane of our universe, the āḍi-ṭaṭṭva plane, it may be of interest to explain how it is possible for them to see what may very probably be the atom of that plane. That this may be understood it is essential to remember that the power of magnification by means of which these experiments are conducted is quite apart from the faculty of functioning upon one or other of the planes. The latter is the result of a slow and gradual unfoldment of the Self, while the former is merely a special development of one of the many powers latent in man. All the planes are round us here, just as much as any other point in space, and if a man sharpens his sight until he can see their tiniest atoms he can make a study of them, even though he may as yet be far from the level necessary to enable him to understand and function upon the higher planes as a whole, or to come into touch with the glorious Intelligences who gather those atoms into vehicles for Themselves.

A partial analogy may be found in the position of the astronomer with regard to the stellar universe, or let us say the Milky Way. He can observe its constituent parts and learn a good deal about them along various lines, but it is absolutely impossible for him to see it as a whole from outside, or to form any certain conception of its true shape, and to know what it really is. Suppose that the universe is, as many of the ancients thought, some inconceivably vast Being, it is utterly impossible for us, here in the midst of it, to know what that Being is or is doing, for that would mean raising ourselves to a height comparable with His ; but we may make extensive and detailed examination of such particles of His body as happen to be within our reach, for that means only the patient use of powers and machinery already at our command.

Let it not be supposed that, in thus unfolding a little more of the wonders of Divine Truth by pushing our investigations to the very furthest point at present possible to us, we in any way alter or modify all that has been written in theosophical books of the shape and constitution of the physical atom, and of the wonderful and orderly arrangements by which it is grouped into the various chemical molecules ; all this remains entirely unaffected.

Nor is any change introduced as regards the three outpourings from the LOGOS, and the marvellous facility with which the matter of the various planes is by them moulded into forms for the service of the evolving life. But if we wish to have a right view of the realities underlying manifestation in this universe, we must to a considerable extent reverse the ordinary conception as to what this matter essentially is. Instead of thinking of its ultimate constituents as solid specks floating in a void, we must realise that it is the apparent void itself which is solid, and that the specks are but bubbles in it. That fact once grasped, all the rest remains as before. The relative position of what we have hitherto called matter and force is still for us the same as ever ; it is only that, on closer examination, both of these conceptions prove to be variants of force, the one ensouling combinations of the other, and the real 'matter,' koilon, is seen to be something which has hitherto been altogether outside our scheme of thought.

In view of this marvellous distribution of Himself in 'space,' the familiar concept of the 'sacrifice of the LOGOS,' takes on a new depth and splendor ; this is His 'dying in matter,' His 'perpetua sacrifice,' and it may be the very glory of the LOGOS that He can sacrifice Himself to the uttermost by thus permeating and making

Himself one with that portion of koilon which He chooses as the field of His universe.

What koilon is, what its origin, whether it is itself changed by the Divine Breath which is poured into it—does 'Dark Space' thus become 'Bright Space' at the beginning of a manifestation ?—these are questions to which we cannot at present even indicate answers. Perchance an intelligent study of the great Scriptures of the world may yield replies.

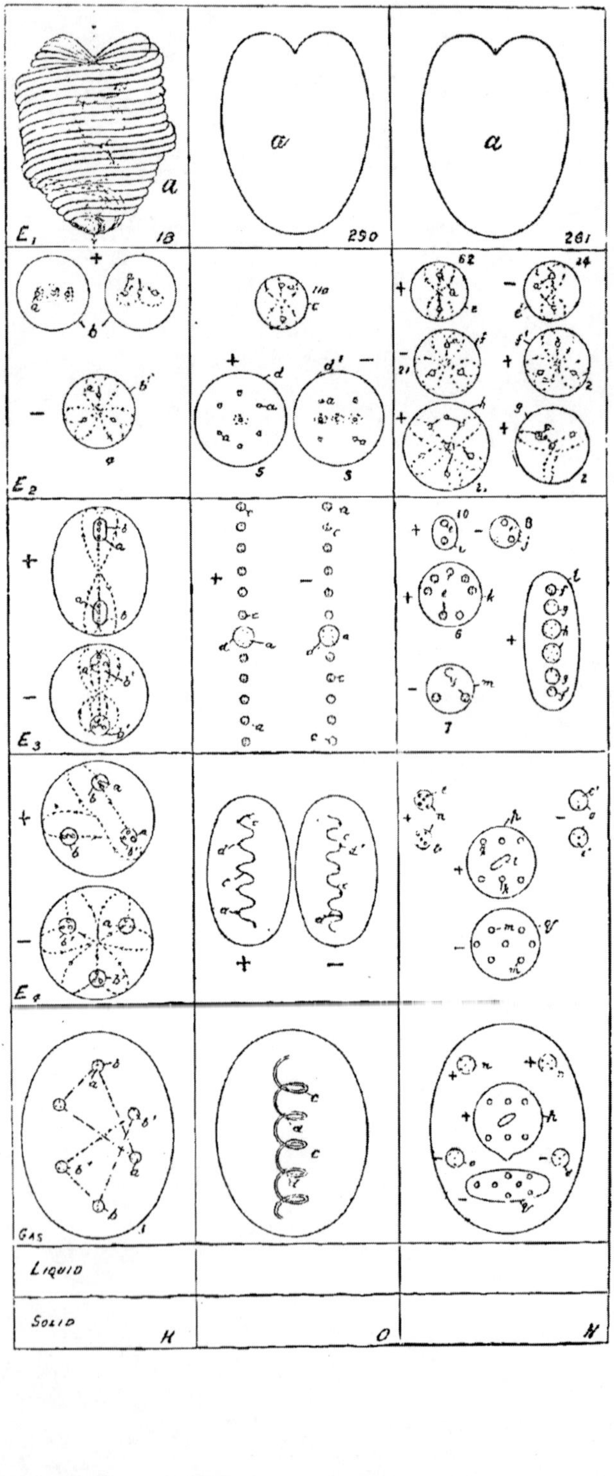

E1
18
290
261
E2
E3
E4
GAS
LIQUID
SOLID
H
O
N

OCCULT CHEMISTRY.*

Of late years there has been much discussion among scientific men as to the genesis of the chemical elements, and as to the existence and constitution of the ether. The apparatus which forms the only instrument of research of the scientists cannot even reach the confines of the ether, and they apparently never dream of the possibility of examining their chemical atom. There is in regard to both atom and ether a wealth of speculation but a poverty of observation—for lack, of course, of any means which would render observation possible.

Now man possesses senses, capable of evolution into activity, that are able to observe beyond the limits of the sensitiveness of the five senses. These latter organs receive vibrations from the physical world, but their capacity of reception is comparatively narrow, and vast numbers of vibrations, still physical in their character, leave them entirely unaffected. The keener and more delicate senses of the astral body are latent for the most part in men of our race, and are therefore not available for general use. Yet they afford instruments for observation on the higher levels of the physical plane, and bring under direct ken objects which from their minuteness or subtlety escape ordinary vision. It seems worth while to lay before the public a few observations made through these senses, partly because it is possible that they may suggest hypotheses useful as elucidating some scientific problems; and partly because science is advancing rapidly and will ere long be investigating some of these matters for itself, and it will then perhaps be well for the Theosophical Society if the first statement of facts that will then be accepted should have come from members of its body.

The physical world is regarded as being composed of between sixty and seventy chemical elements, aggregated into an infinite variety of combinations. These combinations fall under the three main heads of solids, liquids and gases, the recognised substates of physical matter, with the theoretical ether scarcely admitted as material. Ether, to the scientist, is not a substate or even a state of matter, but is a something apart by itself. It would not be allowed that gold could be raised to the etheric condition as it might be to

* This is reprinted from *Lucifer* of November, 1895.

the liquid and gaseous ; whereas the occultist knows that the gaseous is succeeded by the etheric, as the solid is succeeded by the liquid, and he knows also that the word "ether" covers four substates as distinct from each other as are the solids, liquids and gases, and that all chemical elements have their four etheric substates the highest being common to all, and consisting of the ultimate physical atoms to which all elements are finally reducible. The chemical atom is regarded as the ultimate particle of any element, and is supposed to be indivisible and unable to exist in a free state. Mr. Crookes' researches have led the more advanced chemists to regard the atoms as compound, as a more or less complex aggregation of protyle.

To astral vision ether is a visible thing, and is seen permeating all substances and encircling every particle. A 'solid' body is a body composed of a vast number of particles suspended in ether, each vibrating backwards and forwards in a particular field at a high rate of velocity ; the particles are attracted towards each other more strongly than they are attracted by external influences, and they 'cohere,' or maintain towards each other a definite relation in space. Closer examination shows that the ether is not homogeneous but consists of particles of numerous kinds, differing in the aggregations of the minute bodies composing them ; and a careful and more detailed method of analysis reveals that it has four distinct degrees, giving us, with the solid, liquid and gaseous, seven instead of four substates of matter in the physical world.

These four etheric substates will be best understood if the method be explained by which they were studied. This method consisted of taking what is called an atom of gas, and breaking it up time after time, until what proved to be the ultimate physical atom was reached, the breaking up of this last resulting in the production of astral, and no longer physical matter.

It is, of course, impossible to convey by words the clear conceptions that are gained by direct vision of the objects of study, and the accompanying diagram—cleverly drawn from the description given by the investigators—is offered as a substitute, however poor, for the lacking vision of the readers. The horizontal lines separate from each other the seven substates of matter ; solid, liquid, gas, ether 4, ether 3, ether 2, ether 1. On the gas level are represented three chemical atoms, one of hydrogen (H), one of oxygen (O), one of nitrogen (N). The successive changes undergone by each chemical atom are shown in the compartments vertically above it, the left-hand column showing the breaking up of the hydrogen atom, the middle column that of the oxygen atom, the right-hand column that of the nitrogen atom. The ultimate physical atom is marked *a*, and is drawn only once, although it is the same throughout. The numbers 18, 290 and 261 are the numbers of the ultimate physical atoms found to exist in a chemical atom.

The dots indicate the lines along which force is observed to be playing, and the arrowheads show the direction of the force. No attempt has been made to show this below E 2 except in the case of the hydrogen. The letters given are intended to help the reader to trace upwards any special body ; thus *d* in the oxygen chemical atom on the gas level may be found again on E 4, E 3, and E 2. It must be remembered that the bodies shown diagrammatically in no way indicate relative size ; as a body is raised from one substate to the one immediately above it, it is enormously magnified for the purpose of investigation, and the ultimate atom on E 1 is represented by the dot *a* on the gaseous level.

The first chemical atom selected for this examination was an atom of hydrogen (H). On looking carefully at it, it was seen to consist of six small bodies, contained in an egg-like form. It rotated with great rapidity on its own axis, vibrating at the same time, and the internal bodies performed similar gyrations. The whole atom spins and quivers, and has to be steadied before exact observation is possible. The six little bodies are arranged in two sets of three, forming two triangles that are not interchangeable, but are related to each other as object and image. (The lines in the diagram of it on the gaseous sub-plane are not lines of force, but show the two triangles ; on a plane surface the interpenetration of the triangles cannot be clearly indicated). Futher, the six bodies are not all alike ; they each contain three smaller bodies—each of these being an ultimate physical atom—but in two of them the three atoms are arranged in a line, while in the remaining four they are arranged in a triangle.

The wall of the limiting spheroid in which the bodies are enclosed being composed of the matter of the third, or gaseous, kind, drops away when the gaseous atom is raised to the next level, and the six bodies are set free. They at once re-arrange themselves in two triangles, each enclosed by a limiting sphere ; the two marked *b* in the diagram unite with one of those marked *b′* to form a body which shows a positive character, the remaining three forming a second body negative in type. These form the hydrogen particles of the lowest plane of ether, marked E 4—ether 4—on the diagram. On raising these further, they undergo another disintegration, losing their limiting walls ; the positive body of E 4, on losing its wall, becomes two bodies, one consisting of the two particles, marked *b*, distinguishable by the linear arrangement of the contained ultimate atoms, enclosed in a wall, and the other being the third body enclosed in E 4 and now set free. The negative body of E 4 similarly, on losing its wall, becomes two bodies, one consisting of the two particles marked *b′*, and the second the remaining body, being set free. These free bodies do not remain on E 3 but pass immediately to E 2, leaving the positive and negative bodies, each containing two particles, as the representatives of hydrogen on E 3. On taking these bodies a step higher their wall disappears, and the internal bodies are set free, those containing the atoms arranged lineally being positive, and those with the triangular arrangement being negative. These two forms represent hydrogen on E 2, but similar bodies of this state of matter are found entering into other combinations, as may be seen by referring to *f* on E 2 of nitrogen (N). On raising these bodies yet one step further, the falling away of the walls sets the contained atoms free, and we reach the ultimate physical atom, the matter of E I. The disintegration of this sets free particles of astral matter, so that we have reached in this the limit of physical matter. The Theosophical reader will notice with interest that we can thus observe seven distinct substates of physical matter, and no more.

The ultimate atom, which is the same in all the observed cases, is an exceedingly complex body, and only its main characteristics are given in the diagram. It is composed entirely of spirals, the spiral being in its turn composed of spirillæ, and these again of minuter spirillæ. A fairly accurate drawing is given in Babbitt's *Principles of Light and Colour*, p. 102. The illustrations there given of atomic combinations are entirely wrong and misleading, but if the stove-pipe run through the centre of the single atom be removed, the picture may be taken as correct, and will give some idea of the complexity of this fundamental unit of the physical universe,

Turning to the force side of the atom and its combinations, we observe that force pours into the heart-shaped depression at the top of the atom, and issues from the point, and is changed in character by its passage ; further, force rushes through every spiral and every spirilla, and the changing shades of color that flash out from the rapidly revolving and vibrating atom depend on the several activities of the spirals ; sometimes one, sometimes another, is thrown into more energetic action, and with the change of activity from one spiral to another the color changes.

The building of a gaseous atom of hydrogen may be traced downward from E 1, and, as said above, the lines given in the diagram are intended to indicate the play of the forces which bring about the several combinations. Speaking generally, positive bodies are marked by their contained atoms setting their points towards each other and the centre of their combination, and repelling each other outwards ; negative bodies are marked by the heart-shaped depressions being turned inwards, and by a tendency to move towards each other instead of away. Every combination begins by a welling up of force at a centre, which is to form the centre of the combination ; in the first positive hydrogen combination, E 2, an atom revolving at right angles to the plane of the paper—turning head over heels, if the expression may be allowed—and also revolving on its own axis, forms the centre, and force, rushing out at its lower point, rushes in at the depressions of two other atoms, which then set themselves with their points to the centre ; the lines are shown in + b, right-hand figure. (The left-hand figure indicates the revolution of the atoms each by itself). As this atomic triad whirls round, it clears itself a space, pressing back the undifferentiated matter of the plane, and making to itself a whirling wall of this matter, thus taking the first step towards building up the chemical hydrogen atom. A negative atomic triad is similarly formed, the three atoms being symmetrically arranged round the centre of out-welling force. These atomic triads then combine, two of the linear arrangement being attracted to each other, and two of the triangular, force again welling up and forming a centre and acting on the triads as on a single atom, and a limiting wall being again formed as the combination revolves round its centre. The next stage is produced by each of these combinations on E 3 attracting to itself a third atomic triad of the triangular type from E 2, by the setting up of a new centre of up-welling force, following the lines traced in the combinations of E 4. Two of these uniting, and their triangles interpenetrating, the chemical atom is formed, and we find it to contain in all eighteen ultimate physical atoms.

The next substance investigated was oxygen, a far more complicated and puzzling body; the difficulties of observation were very much increased by the extraordinary activity shown by this element and the dazzling brilliancy of some of its constituents. The gaseous atom is an ovoid body, within which a spirally coiled snake-like body revolves at a high velocity, five brilliant points of light shining on the coils. The snake appears to be a solid rounded body, but on raising the atom to E 4 the snake splits lengthwise into two waved bodies, and it is seen that the appearance of solidity is due to the fact that these spin round a common axis in opposite directions, and so present a continuous surface, as a ring of fire can be made by whirling a lighted stick. The brilliant bodies seen in the atom are on the crests of the waves in the positive snake, and in the hollows in the negative one; the snake itself consists of small bead-like bodies, eleven of which interpose between the larger brilliant spots. On raising these bodies to E 3 the snakes break up, each bright spot carrying with it six beads on one side and five on the other; these twist and writhe about still with the same extraordinary activity, reminding one of fire-flies stimulated to wild gyrations. It can be seen that the larger brilliant bodies each enclose seven ultimate atoms, while the beads each enclose two. (Each bright spot with its eleven beads is enclosed in a wall, accidentally omitted in the diagram). On the next stage, E 2, the fragments of the snakes break up into their constituent parts; the positive and negative bodies, marked *d* and *d'*, showing a difference of arrangement of the atoms contained in them. These again finally disintegrate, setting free the ultimate physical atoms, identical with those obtained from hydrogen. The number of ultimate atoms contained in the gaseous atom of oxygen is 290, made up as follows:

2 in each bead, of which there are 110;

7 in each bright spot, of which there are 10;

$2 \times 110 + 70 = 290$.

When the observers had worked out this, they compared it with the number of ultimate atoms in hydrogen :

$$18)\overline{290}$$

$$16{\cdot}11+$$

The respective numbers of ultimate atoms contained in a chemical atom of these two bodies are thus seen to closely correspond with their accepted weight-numbers.

It may be said in passing that a chemical atom of ozone appears as an oblate spheroid, with the contained spiral much compressed and widened in the centre ; the spiral consists of three snakes, one positive and two negative, formed in a single revolving body. On raising the chemical atom to the next plane, the snake divides into three, each being enclosed in its own egg.

The chemical atom of nitrogen was the third selected by the students for examination, as it seemed comparatively quiet in contrast with the ever-excited oxygen. It proved, however, to be the most complicated of all in its internal arrangements, and its quiet was therefore a little deceptive. Most prominent was the balloon-shaped body in the middle, with six smaller bodies in two horizontal rows and one large egg-shaped one in the midst, contained in it. Some chemical atoms were seen in which the internal arrangement of these contained bodies was changed and the two horizontal rows became vertical ; this change seemed to be connected with a greater activity of the whole body, but the observations on this head are too incomplete to be reliable. The balloon-shaped body is positive, and is apparently drawn downwards towards the negative egg-shaped body below it, containing seven smaller particles. In addition to these large bodies, four small ones are seen, two positive and two negative, the positive containing five and the negative four minuter spots. On raising the gaseous atom to E 4, the falling away of the wall sets free the six contained bodies, and both the balloon and the egg round themselves, apparently with the removal of their propinquity, as though they had exercised over each other some attractive influence. The smaller bodies within the egg—marked *q* on E 4—are not on one plane, and those within *n* and *o* form respectively square-based and triangular based pyramids. On raising all these bodies to E 3 we find the walls fall away as usual, and the contents of each 'cell' are set free : *p* of E 4 contains six small bodies marked *k*, and these are shown in *k* of E 3, as containing each seven little bodies—marked *e*—each of which has within it two ultimate atoms ; the long form of *p* E 4—marked *l*—appears as the long form *l* on E 3, and this has three pairs of smaller bodies within it, *f'*, *g* and *h*, containing respectively three, four and six ultimate atoms ; *q* of E 4, with its seven contained particles, *m*, has three particles *m* on E 3, each showing three ultimate atoms within them ; *e* from *n* of E 4 becomes *i* of E 3, with contained bodies, *e*, showing two ultimate atoms in each ; while *e'* from *o* of E 4 becomes *j* of E 3, each having three smaller bodies within it, *e'*, with two ultimate atoms in each. On E 2, the arrangement of these ultimate atoms is shown, and the pairs *f'*, *g* and *h* are seen with the lines of force indicated ; the triads in *f*—from *m* of E 3—are similarly shown, and the duads in *e* and *e'*—from *i* and *j* of E 3—are given in the same way. When all these bodies are raised to E 1, the ultimate physical atoms are set free, identical, of course, with that previously described. Reckoning up the number of ultimate physical atoms in a chemical atom of nitrogen we find they amount to 261, thus divided :

62 +	bodies	with	2	ultimate	atoms,	62 × 2 = 124
24 −	"	"	2	"	"	24 × 2 = 48
21 −	"	"	3	"	"	21 × 3 = 63
2 +	"	"	3	"	"	2 × 3 = 6
2 +	"	"	4	"	"	2 × 4 = 8
2 +	"	"	4	"	"	2 × 6 = 12
						261

This again approaches closely the weight-number assigned to nitrogen ;

18) 261

14·44 +

This is interesting as checking the observations, for weight-numbers are arrived at in so very different a fashion, and especially in the case of nitrogen the approximation is noteworthy, from the complexity of the bodies which yield the number on analysis.

Some other observations were made which went to show that as weight-numbers increased, there was a corresponding increase in the number of bodies discerned within the chemical atom ; thus, gold showed 47 contained bodies ; but these observations need repetition and checking. Investigation of a molecule of water revealed the presence of twelve bodies from hydrogen and the characteristic snake of oxygen, the encircling walls of the chemical atoms being broken away But here again, further observations are necessary to substantiate details. The present paper is only offered as a suggestion of an inviting line of research, promising interesting results of a scientific character ; the observations recorded have been repeated several times and are not the work of a single investigator, and they are believed to be correct so far as they go.

THE PLATONIC SOLIDS.

Some of our readers may be glad to have a drawing of the Platonic solids, since they play so large a part in the building up of elements. The regular solids are five, and five only ; in each :

1. The lines are equal.
2. The angles are equal.
3. The surfaces are equal.

It will be seen that the tetrahedron is the fundamental form, the three-sided pyramid on a triangular base, *i.e.*, a solid figure formed

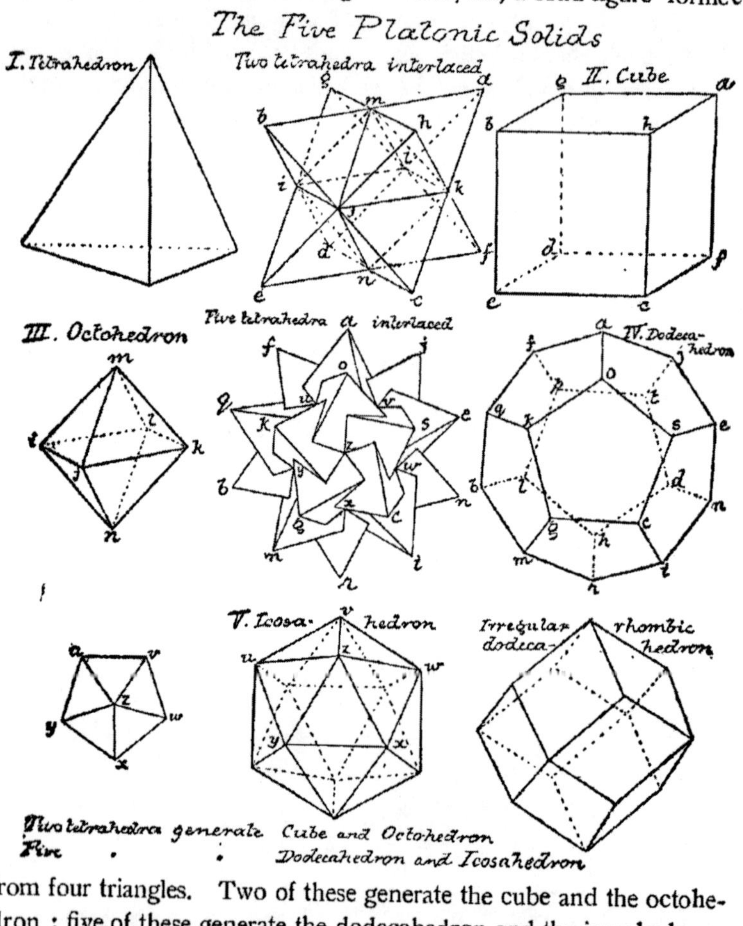

from four triangles. Two of these generate the cube and the octohedron ; five of these generate the dodecahedron and the icosahedron.

The rhombic dodecahedron is not regular, for though the lines and surfaces are equal, the angles are not.

NOTES.

Mr. C. Jinarājadāsa writes :

The asterisk put before metargon in the list of elements should be omitted, for metargon had been discovered by Sir William Ramsey and Mr. Travers at the same time as neon (see *Proc. of the Royal Society*, Vol. LXIII, p. 411), and therefore before it was observed clairvoyantly. It is not, however, given in the latest list of elements in the Report of November 13, 1907, of the International Atomic Weights Commission, so it would seem as though it were not yet fully recognised.

Neon was discovered in 1898 by Ramsey and Travers, and the weight given to it was 22. This almost corresponds with our weight for meta-neon, 22·33 ; the latest weight given to neon is 20, and that corresponds within $\frac{1}{10}$th to our weight, 19·9. From this it would seem that neon was examined in the later investigations and meta-neon in the earlier.

He says further on a probable *fourth* Interperiodic Group :

Thinking over the diagrams, it seemed to me likely that a fourth group exists, coming on the paramagnetic side, directly under iron, cobalt, nickel, just one complete swing of the pendulum after rhodium, ruthenium, palladium. This would make four interperiodic groups, and they would come also *periodically* in the table too.

I took the diagram for Osmium, and in a bar postulated only three columns for the first element of the new groups *i.e.*, one column less than in Osmium. This would make 183 atoms in a bar ; the new group then would follow in a bar , 183, 185, 187. Here I found to my surprise that the third postulated group would have a remarkable relation to Os. Ir. Pt.

Thus

Os.—245	(in a bar) ;	less 60 = 185
Ir. 247		less 60 = 187
Pt. 249		less 60 = 189

But strange to say *also*

Ruthenium (bar)	132	less 60—72
Rhodium	134	less 60—74
Palladium	136	less 60—76.

But 72, 74, 76, are Iron, Cobalt and Nickel.

So there does probably exist a new group with bars (183), 185, 187, 189, with atomic weights.

X = bar 185 ;		atoms	2590, wt. 143·3
Y =	187,		2618, wt. 145·4
Z =	189,		2646, wt. 147·0.

They come probably among the rare earths. Probably also Neodymium and Praseodymium are two of them, for their weights are 143·6, 140·5.

Thompson & Co., Printers Madras.

INDEX.

PAGE.

Aluminium ... 14, 55, 56, 57, 61, 62, 88
Antimony ... 14, 57, 58, 59, 63, 64, 88
Argon ... 13, 83, 85, 86
Arsenic ... 14, 57, 58, 60
Atom, two types ... 5, 8
„ construction ... 6
„ effect of electricity on ... 7
„ ultimate physical ... 5, 15
„ wall of ... 6, 7, 26

Balloon ... 21, 24, 26, 28, 29, 51, 52, 53, 59, 60, 61, 74, 75, 76, 82, 83, 84, 85, 86, 87
Barium ... 35
Bars ... 14, 70, 71
Beryllium ... 10, 13, 35, 36, 37, 43, 44, 46
Boron ... 10, 13, 50, 51, 59, 61
Bromine ... 13, 15, 16, 17, 18, 20, 22 24, 29, 31, 32

Cadmium 13, 39, 40, 41, 48, 49, 89, 90, 91

Calcium 13, 35, 36, 37, 38, 43, 44, 46, 89
Carbon ... 10, 64, 65, 66, 77, 79
Chlorine ... 13, 16, 17, 18, 19, 20, 22, 29, 30, 31, 32, 33, 35, 37, 44
Chromium ... 13, 35, 36, 38, 45, 46, 89
' Cigar ' (or prism) ... 22, 24, 28, 33, 35, 36, 37, 44, 50, 51, 52, 54, 55, 56, 59, 60, 61, 62, 64, 65, 66, 67, 68 77, 78, 79, 80, 81, 83, 85, 90, 91
Cobalt ... 14, 69, 70, 71, 80, 81, 83
Cone ... 21, 22, 23, 24, 25, 33, 34, 39, 40, 41, 42, 47, 48, 67, 68, 70, 71, 72, 73, 74, 80, 81, 82, 91
Copper ... 12, 19, 21, 22, 23, 29,
Counting of atoms ... 3
Cæsium ... 70
Cross ... 28, 32, 34, 39, 40, 43, 47, 48, 50, 60, 63, 64, 65, 74, 77, 78, 79, 80, 90
Cube ... 13, 14, 15, 39, 40, 50

Discoveries of new elements ... 2
Dodecahedron ... 15
Dumb-bell ... 2, 12, 13, 17, 19, 21, 22, 23

Elements, list of ... 4
„ groupings of ... 12, 15
Examination, method of ... 2

PAGE.

Fluorine ... 10, 11, 14 15, 68, 69, 70, 74, 76, 83

Gallium ... 14, 55, 56, 61, 62
Germanium ... 13, 14, 64, 67, 68, 80
Glucinum (see Beryllium) ...
Gold ... 2, 3, 12, 13, 17, 22, 23-25, 29, 33—35, 37, 47, 60

Helium ... 2, 10, 11, 13, 14, 17 (note) 84, 85
Hydrogen... 1, 2, 3, 13, 14, 15, 16, 17, 19, 27, 28, 88

Icosahedron ... 15
Indium ... 14, 55, 56, 57, 58, 62
Interperiodic groups ... 69, 70
Iodine ... 13, 15, 16, 17, 18, 20, 22, 24, 32, 33, 34, 35, 61
Iridium ... 14, 68, 69, 70, 72, 73
Iron ... 2, 10, 11, 14, 22, 24, 69, 70, 71 80, 81, 82

Kalon ... 2, 13, 83, 86, 87, 88
Krypton ... 13, 83, 84, 86, 87

Lithium 10, 11, 14, 15, 70, 74, 75, 82 83, 91,

Magnesium ... 13, 39, 40, 46, 47, 48, 90
Manganese ... 14, 69, 74, 75, 83
Matter, states of ... 8—11, 17
Mercury ... 39
Meta-kalon ... 2, 13, , 83, 87, 88
Metargon ... 13, 83, 85, 86
Metakrypton ... 13, 83, 86, 87
Metaneon ... 13, 83, 85, 85
Metaxenon ... 13, 83, 87
Molybdenum... 13, 35, 36, 37, 38, 39, 45, 46, 89, 91

Neon ... 13, 14, 83, 85, 85
Nickel ... 14, 69, 70, 71, 80, 81
Niobium ... 14 50, 53, 54, 55, 61, 84
Nitrogen .. 1, 11, 14, 17, 18, 50, 51, 52, 53, 54, 61, 74, 82, 84, 86

Occultum ...2, 13, 21, 25, 26, 28, 34, 78
Octahedron ... 14, 15, 64, 77
Osmium ... 2, 14, 69, 70, 72, 73, 81
Ovoid of 63 atoms ... 51, 52, 53, 54, 60

PAGE.

Oxygen... 1, 13, 14, 17, 18, 36, 37, 38, 45, 46

Palladium ... 14, 69, 70, 71, 72, 81
Phosphorus ... 14, 57, 58, 63
Platinum 14, 22, 68, 69, 70, 72, 73, 82
Potassium ... 14, 74, 75, 82
Prism (see cone) ...

Radium ... 88, 89, 90, 91, 92
Ring ... 21, 24, 25, 28, 34
Rhodium ...14, 69, 70, 71, 72, 81
Rubidium .. 11, 14, 70, 74, 75, 76, 82, 83
Ruthenium ... 14, 69, 70, 71, 72, 81

Scandium ... 14, 50, 51, 52, 59, 60
Selenium... 11, 13, 39, 41, 42, 48, 49, 90
Silicon ... 14, 64, 67, 79, 81, 82
Silver ... 2, 12, 19, 21, 22, 23, 24, 29, 33, 34, 68, 73, 80, 81, 82
Sodium ... 2, 3, 10, 11, 12, 19, 21, 22, 29, 30, 78, 79, 80
Spikes ... 39, 41, 47, 48, 68, 74, 80, 83, 90, 91
Stars ... 14, 83, 86
" floating ... 13, 41
Strontium ... 13, 35, 36, 37, 38, 39, 46 89, 91
Sulphur ... 13, 39, 41, 42, 48

PAGE.

Tellurium ... 13, 39, 42, 43, 48, 49, 50
Tetrahedron ... 13, 15, 16, 24, 25, 26, 28, 32, 33, 35, 38, 39, 46, 51, 52, 54, 55, 61, 63, 65, 66, 67, 68, 74, 78, 80, 82, 83, 85, 86, 87, 88, 91
Tin ... 2, 13, 14, 22, 64, 67, 68, 73, 79, 80
Titanium ... 13, 14, 25, 64, 65, 66, 77, 78, 79, 80, 81
Types of hyper-meta-proto elements... 9
" " meta-proto-elements ... 10
" " proto elements ... 11

Uranium .. 35, 37

Vanadium ... 14, 50, 53, 54, 55, 61, 84

Wolfram ... 35, 37

Xenon ... 2, 13, 83, 86, 87

Yttrium ... 13, 14, 50, 52, 53, 60, 61, 84

Zenon (xenon) ...
Zinc ... 2, 13, 22, 39, 40, 41, 47, 48, 68, 80, 89, 91
Zirconium 13, 14, 64, 65, 66, 77, 78, 79